AS/A-LEVEL

STUDENT GUIDE

AQA

Geography

Component 3:

Hazards; Population and
the environment

David Redfern

Hodder Education, an Hachette UK company, Blenheim Court, George Street, Banbury, Oxfordshire OX16 5BH

Orders
Bookpoint Ltd, 130 Milton Park, Abingdon, Oxfordshire OX14 4SB

tel: 01235 827827

fax: 01235 400401

e-mail: education@bookpoint.co.uk

Lines are open 9.00 a.m.–5.00 p.m., Monday to Saturday, with a 24-hour message answering service. You can also order through the Hodder Education website: www.hoddereducation.co.uk

© David Redfern 2017

ISBN 978-1-4718-6418-6

First printed 2017

Impression number 5 4 3 2 1

Year 2021 2020 2019 2018 2017

Cover photo: pure-life-pictures/Fotolia

Typeset by Integra Software Services Pvt Ltd, Pondicherry, India

Printed in Italy

Hachette UK's policy is to use papers that are natural, renewable and recyclable products and made from wood grown in sustainable forests. The logging and manufacturing processes are expected to conform to the environmental regulations of the country of origin.

Contents

■ Getting the most from this book

Questions & Answers

Student answer

Japan sits on two continental plates — the northern part of the country lies on the North American Plate, while the south is on the Eurasian Plate. To the east of Japan are two oceanic plates — in the north is the Pacific Plate, and to the south lies the Philippine Plate. The two oceanic plates are both moving in a generally westward direction at a rate of a few centimetres per year. The zones at which the plates collide lie on the seabed to the east of Japan (Figure 1a) and are marked by deep ocean trenches. At this point the oceanic plates are being forced under the continental plates (known as subduction) and earthquakes take place along such a tectonic boundary 🖉

The earthquake off Sendai in Tohoku in 2011 occurred on the fault that marks the boundary between the Pacific Plate to the east and the North American Plate to the west — 130 km to the east of the port of Sendai. The impact of the earthquake, as measured by the MMI scale on Figure 1b, was greatest all along the 400 km east coastline of Tohoku in a thin band parallel to the coast, north and south of Sendai. The intensity then reduced inland and to the west in a fairly uniform manner, and it also decreased to the southwest. There is, therefore, a strong relation of the intensity of the earthquake to the tectonic setting 🖉

ⓔ 5/6 marks awarded. 🖉 The student begins with an excellent description of the tectonic setting, making use of both plate names and directions of movement, and making sensible suggestions of both landforms and processes. The background to the earthquake is therefore well explained. The second paragraph then moves on to the second part of the question — linkage to the intensity of the earthquake — by describing the pattern of earthquake intensity. 🖉 The final sentence makes clear the link that exists, and therefore the answer is integrated. It is a pity that the student did not explore some of the complexities of the relationship, perhaps by commenting on the linear shape of the pattern of intensity. Mid-Level 2 awarded.

Question 3

(Note how this question makes links between two separate areas of the specification, Hazards and Global governance.)

Assess the importance of governance in the successful management of tectonic hazards.   [9 marks]

ⓔ Mark scheme:
■ Level 3 (7–9 marks):
 – AO1: demonstrates detailed knowledge and understanding of concepts, processes, interactions and change. These underpin the response throughout.
 – AO2: applies knowledge and understanding appropriately and with detail. Detailed evidence of the drawing together of a range of geographical ideas, which is used constructively to support the response. Assessment is detailed and well supported with appropriate evidence. A well-balanced and coherent argument is presented.

62   AQA Geography

Sample student answers

Practise the questions, then look at the student answers that follow.

Exam-style questions

Commentary on the questions

Tips on what you need to do to gain full marks, indicated by the icon ⓔ

Commentary on sample student answers

Read the comments (preceded by the icon ⓔ) showing how many marks each answer would be awarded in the exam and exactly where marks are gained or lost.

■ About this book

Much of the knowledge and understanding needed for AS and A-level geography builds on what you have learned for GCSE geography, but with an added focus on key geographical concepts and depth of knowledge and understanding of content. This guide offers advice for the effective revision of Hazards, which many students may need to complete for AS and A-level, and Population and the environment, which only some A-level students may complete.

In the AS Paper 1 external exam, Section B tests your knowledge and application of aspects of Hazards or Contemporary urban environments. (The latter and Section A are not covered in this guide.) The whole exam lasts 1 hour and 30 minutes, and the unit makes up 50% of the AS award. In the A-level Paper 1 external exam, Section C tests Hazards or Ecosystems under stress. (The latter and Sections A and B are not covered in this guide.) The whole exam lasts 2 hours and 30 minutes, and the unit makes up 40% of the A-level award.

In the A-level Paper 2 external exam, Section C tests Population and the environment or Contemporary urban environments or Resource security. (Only the first topic is covered in this guide.) The whole exam lasts 2 hours and 30 minutes, and the unit makes up 40% of the A-level award. More information on the exam papers is given in the Questions & Answers section (pages 56–92).

To be successful in this unit you have to understand:
■ the key ideas of the content
■ the nature of the assessment material — by reviewing and practising sample structured questions
■ how to achieve a high level of performance within them

This guide has two sections:

Content Guidance: this summarises some of the key information that you need to know to be able to answer the examination questions with a high degree of accuracy and depth. In particular, the meaning of keys terms is made clear and some attention is paid to providing details of case study material to help to meet the spatial context requirement within the specification.

Questions & Answers: this includes some sample questions similar in style to those you might expect in the exam. There are some sample student responses to these questions as well as detailed analysis, which will give further guidance in relation to what exam markers are looking for to award top marks.

The best way to use this book is to read through the relevant topic area first before practising the questions. Only refer to the answers and examiner comments after you have attempted the questions.

Content Guidance

This section outlines the following areas of the AQA AS and A-level geography specifications:

- Hazards (AS and A-level)
- Population and the environment (A-level only)

Read through the chosen topic area(s) before attempting questions from the Question & Answers section.

■ Hazards

The concept of hazard in a geographical context

Nature, forms and potential impacts of hazards

A hazard is defined as a perceived natural/geophysical event that has the potential to threaten both life and property. A hazard has impacts that are social (loss of life and injury), economic (property damage, employment prospects and community loss) and environmental. A geophysical event would not be hazardous without some human occupancy of the location affected.

There are a number of different types of hazards.

- **Geophysical:** all the tectonic hazards of volcanoes, earthquakes and tsunami
- **Hydrological:** essentially the extremes of wet weather, i.e. droughts and floods
- **Atmospheric:** tropical storms (known by a variety of names — hurricanes, typhoons, cyclones and willy-willies), tornadoes and extra-tropical storms (such as deep depressions affecting the British Isles)
- **Geomorphic:** landslides and avalanches
- **Biohazards:** wildfires and locust plagues
- **Multiple hazardous zones:** places that experience a combination of the above

Few hazards are entirely natural. Their relationship with disaster is the result of human **vulnerability**. Some hazards, such as wildfires, can be naturally occurring, or they can be caused by the direct or indirect impact of human actions — deliberately setting vegetation alight or carelessness. In many cases, human actions intensify the impact of natural hazards, for example exacerbating earthquake risk by building inappropriate buildings.

A **disaster** is the realisation of a hazard, when it causes a 'significant impact' on a vulnerable population. It causes serious disruption of the functioning of a community or society, involving widespread/serious socioeconomic and environmental losses

Knowledge check 1

Distinguish between the primary and secondary effects of a hazard.

Vulnerability The risk of exposure to hazards combined with an inability to cope with them.

that exceed the ability of the community (local/national) to cope. In other words, it exceeds their capacity and resilience level.

Risk is the probability of a hazard occurring and creating a loss of lives and/or livelihoods. It might be assumed that risk to a hazard is involuntary, but in reality many people consciously place themselves at risk. Consider, for example, all the people who live in the shadow of volcanoes. **Risk assessment** defines the likelihood of harm and damage. For this we should consider the probability of an event occurring and the severity of the hazard when it does occur. If both are high, then the disaster is likely to be greater in magnitude.

Vulnerability implies a high risk of exposure to hazards combined with an inability to cope with them. In human terms it is the degree of resistance offered by a social system to the impact of a hazardous event. In turn this depends on the resilience of the individuals and communities, and the reliability and functioning of management systems that have been put in place to deal with the event. Poverty and low economic status can amplify vulnerability.

Hence the relationship between environmental hazards and the potential impacts on the people and areas affected is a very complex one. When examining the impact of any such event, you should always consider its magnitude, duration and extent, but also the degree to which the people affected can cope and respond. The former are inherently physical in nature, whereas the latter are more functions of the human geography of the area affected.

Hazard perception

People react to the threat of hazards in different ways because of the way in which individuals receive and process information, in turn based on their economic and cultural background. Perception is influenced by many factors including:

- socioeconomic status
- level of education
- occupation and employment status
- religion
- ethnicity
- family and marital status
- past experience
- values, attitudes and expectations

Perception of a hazard will ultimately determine the course of action taken by individuals in order to modify the event or the responses they expect from governments and other organisations.

There is often a great difference in the perception of a hazard between peoples of differing levels of economic development. In wealthier areas there is a sense that the better you are prepared, the more able you will be able to withstand the impact of the hazard and perhaps even prevent the disaster from taking place. This is usually based upon government and community action, and is backed by capital that will fund technology-based solutions. The sense of helplessness in the face of natural hazards tends to increase with the level of poverty and the deprivation of the people. Even in

---

Resilience The degree to which a population or environment can absorb a hazardous event and yet remain within the same state of organisation, i.e. its ability to cope with stress and recover.

Knowledge check 2

Explain how the level of risk can change over time.

wealthier countries there are groups of disadvantaged people who tend to look upon natural hazards as part of their way of life as they are seen as unavoidable, just as the bulk of people in poorer countries see the impacts of these events as being part of the conditions of poverty.

The way people perceive natural hazards can be classified into the following:

- **Fatalism (acceptance):** such hazards are natural events that are part of living in an area. Some communities would go as far as to say that they are 'God's will'. Action is therefore usually concerned with safety first. Losses are accepted as inevitable and people remain where they are.
- **Adaptation/adjustment**: people see that they can prepare for, and therefore survive, the event(s) by **prediction**, prevention and/or protection depending upon the economic and technological circumstances of the area in question.
- **Fear:** the perception of the hazard is such that people feel so vulnerable to an event that they are no longer able to face living in the area, and move away to regions perceived to be safe.

Factors influencing the relationship between hazard and disaster

The factors leading to disaster can be related to both the physical profile of the hazard event and the human context in which it occurs.

Physical factors

Magnitude

Magnitude (the size of the event) is perhaps the key physical factor, but the correlation between magnitude and level of disaster is far from direct. Earthquake magnitude is now measured by the logarithmic moment magnitude scale (MMS), a modification of the earlier Richter scale. The damaging effects are measured by the Mercalli scale (useful for the impacts of shaking).

Volcano magnitude is measured by the Volcanic Explosivity Index (VEI), based on the volume and column height of ejections. This index is very closely related to the type of magma that influences the type of eruption. This can be related back to the type of plate boundary on which the volcano is located. Effusive eruptions of basaltic lavas with low VEI are associated with constructive margins or plumes, whereas explosive eruptions (with high VEI) of andesitic or rhyolitic lava are associated with destructive margins.

The term 'intensity' is often used when describing the magnitude of a tropical storm, and relates to the low level of atmospheric pressure within the storm.

Frequency

Frequency refers to how often an event occurs and is sometimes called the recurrence interval, such as 'a one in 100-year event'. For most hazards there is usually an inverse relationship between frequency and magnitude. The effect of frequency on severity of impact is difficult to gauge but theoretically, areas experiencing frequent tectonic events usually have a plethora of both adaptation and **mitigation** measures, ranging from extensive monitoring, education and community awareness of what to do (for

Adaptation/adjustment The changing of lifestyles or behaviours to cope with the threats and impacts before and after a hazardous event.

Prediction The ability to give warnings so that action can be taken to reduce the impact of hazard events. Improved monitoring and use of ICT have meant that predicting hazards and issuing warnings have become more important.

Mitigation The reduction of the amount and scale of threat and damage caused by a hazardous event.

example, public education programmes, practice of evacuation procedures, the storage of emergency medical and food supplies, and planning for their delivery), to various technological strategies for shockproof building design (e.g. in Tokyo, Japan and San Francisco, USA) or protection (e.g. Japanese tsunami walls).

Duration

Duration refers to the length of time that a hazard exists. Often the initial event is followed by aftershocks (e.g. Christchurch, New Zealand) or a series of subsequent eruptions (e.g. Mt Merapi, Indonesia). While individual earthquakes often last for only 30 seconds, the damage can be very extensive. Secondary hazards often prolong the duration and the damage. For example, the 'triple whammy' of the 2011 Tohoku (Japan) multi-disaster (earthquake, tsunami and nuclear accident) or the secondary hazards associated with volcanic eruptions such as lahars (e.g. Mt Pinatubo, Philippines) or jökulhlaups (glacier bursts in Iceland).

Areal extent

This is the size of the area the hazard covers. This can have a very clear impact, as was the case in the Icelandic ash clouds after Eyjafjallajökull in 2012. These disrupted the whole of the northern hemisphere air transport system for a week, leading to widespread economic losses.

Spatial concentration

This refers to the areal distribution of types of hazards over space, such as earthquakes and volcanoes associated with types of plate boundary. In theory, hazardous regions are avoided for permanent settlement, although the opportunities fertile soils provide encourage agricultural settlements, as on the flanks of Mt Merapi and Mt Etna, Italy. Active tectonic landscapes, especially volcanic examples, also encourage tourism. Generally, spatial concentration promotes sound strategies for management of the hazard, and disasters are rare.

Regularity

Regularity refers to the temporal distribution of hazards, which can add to their disaster potential. While **gap theory** can increase the possible prediction of the 'big one', earthquakes are, in reality, very unpredictable. Volcanic eruptions can be hard to predict precisely, even with close monitoring.

Human factors

Economic factors, including level of development

Human vulnerability is closely associated with levels of absolute poverty and the economic gap, or inequality, between rich and poor. Poverty exacerbates disasters (e.g. Haiti, Kashmir). The poorest countries lack money to invest in education, social services, basic infrastructure and technology, all of which help communities to overcome disasters. Economic growth, however, increases economic assets and therefore raises potential risk levels unless managed effectively.

Social factors

World population is growing, especially in developing nations, with higher levels of urbanisation and many people living in dense population concentrations in unsafe

Gap theory Where there has been a 'gap' in time since the last event, then it is more likely to occur in that location.

Knowledge check 3

Explain how the speed of a hazard's onset can be critical.

living settings, such as poorly sited squatter settlements. Some huge cities are very vulnerable to post-earthquake fires, as was the case in Kobe, Japan. Relief, rescue and recovery efforts are very difficult in some areas. For example, in Kashmir following the 2014 India–Pakistan floods, isolation, low temperatures and the region's frontier position complicated relief and recovery. An increasingly ageing population, as in Sichuan, China, escalates vulnerability to the problems associated with emergency evacuation and survival.

Political factors

The lack of strong central government produces a weak organisational structure. Equally, a lack of financial institutions inhibits both disaster mitigation and emergency and post-disaster recovery. A good, strong central government leads to highly efficient rescue, as illustrated in the Sichuan earthquake, China.

Technological factors

While community preparedness and education can prove absolutely vital in mitigating disasters, technological solutions can play a major role, especially in building design and prevention and protection.

In summary, while the intrinsic physical properties of a hazard's profile can lay the foundations for the development of a disaster, it is the extrinsic human profile that impacts vulnerable communities and societies, and causes disasters. The most vulnerable people, such as those suffering from chronic malnutrition, disease, armed conflict, chaotic and ineffective governance and lack of educational empowerment, are generally channelled into the least resilient environments.

Characteristic human responses

Natural hazards pose a risk to human life, livelihoods and possessions. The response to hazards can occur at a variety of scales, from the individual to the local community, regional, national or international level, and, for large events, at a global scale. The choice of response depends on a complex and interlinked range of physical and human factors (see above). As people and organisations have limited resources and time to make decisions, the relative importance of the physical risk natural hazards pose, compared with other priorities such as providing jobs, education, health services and defence, will be a major factor in influencing how many resources are devoted to reducing the impact of hazards in general.

The following physical factors can affect responses:
- geographical accessibility of the location/region affected
- type of hazard, i.e. scale, impact, magnitude, frequency
- topography of the region affected
- climatic factors

The following human factors can affect responses:
- number of people involved or affected
- degree of community preparedness/risk sharing
- technological resources
- scientific understanding and expertise
- level of general education and training

Exam tip

Note how the above section and the following section interconnect with other parts of the specification (globalisation, governance, urbanisation, population and the character of places). Some questions will require you to make these connections and links.

Community preparedness/risk sharing Involves prearranged measures that aim to reduce the loss of life and property damage through public education and awareness programmes, evacuation procedures, and the provision of emergency medical, food and shelter supplies.

- economic wealth of the region affected
- the quality and quantity of the infrastructure in the area, i.e. roads, railways, airports, health facilities
- the political framework, i.e. government competency and organisation

When taking an overview of hazardous events and their ability to develop into disasters, one approach is to develop a framework of possible strategies. Table 1 illustrates one such framework.

Table 1 The hazard response framework

Strategy	Suggested policies
Modify the loss (adaptation)	■ Provide aid ■ Provide insurance
Modify vulnerability (adaptation)	■ Predict and warn (forecasting) ■ Prepare the community (risk sharing) ■ Educate to change behaviours and prevent hazards becoming disasters
Modify the event (mitigation)	■ Provide some environmental controls to reduce impact ■ Avoid hazards by land-use zoning ■ Design buildings that are hazard resistant ■ Retro-fit buildings to offer some protection
Modify the cause (mitigation)	■ Have total environmental control — prevent the hazard at source (only possible for some small-scale hazards)

The choice of which of these strategies to utilise will vary during the different stages of a hazard, as shown in Park's disaster-response model (see Figure 1). This is an attempt to model the impact of a disaster from before the event to after the event. It also considers the role of emergency relief agencies and rehabilitation. With each hazard event, different areas affected may have a different response curve, as the physical and human factors we saw earlier in this chapter may vary in impact.

> **Exam tip**
>
> Be prepared to apply Park's model to each of the case studies you examine for volcanoes, earthquakes, tropical storms and wildfires. Try to look for both similarities and differences in all of these events.

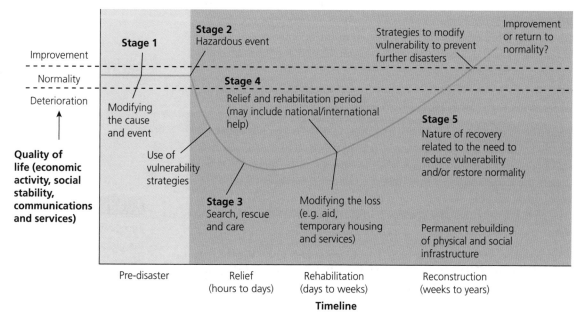

Figure 1 Park's disaster-response model

Park's model is sometimes placed in a circular format, when it is known as the Hazard management cycle (see Figure 2).

Figure 2 The Hazard management cycle

Responses to hazards are controlled by the capability of the people, individuals and groups involved in the management and/or mitigation of those hazards. You should be able to consider and discuss the role of the major players in hazard management, such as governments, non-governmental organisations (NGOs), insurance people, engineers and the media.

Plate tectonics

Earth structure and internal energy sources

The theory of plate tectonics suggests that the Earth's **crust** is split up into seven large, rigid plates and several smaller ones, all of which are able to move slowly on the Earth's surface. They float on the semi-molten **mantle**. Some geoscientists have suggested that the crust/mantle division is more complicated and have introduced new terminology to reflect this:

■ The lithosphere: the crust and upper mantle (80–90 km thick), which form the plates
■ The asthenosphere: the lower part of the mantle

The centre of the Earth (the **core**) is very hot (over 5,000°C), which is caused by both primordial heat and radioactive decay. Some of this heat moves upwards into the asthenosphere as convection currents. As the convection currents slowly move laterally below the Earth's surface, they drag the crust that lies over them. This causes the continental and oceanic plates to move. In addition, this mechanism largely explains the global distribution of volcanoes and earthquakes — they occur mainly at plate margins.

However, it should be pointed out that plate tectonics remains just a theory, because the logistics and cost of drilling down to the Mohorovičić discontinuity (known as 'the Moho') — the boundary between the Earth's crust and the upper mantle, at its thinnest a distance of just 10 km — remain insurmountable.

Exam tip

Familiarise yourself with the global distribution of the major tectonic plates. Most textbooks have maps of their distribution.

Plate tectonic theory and associated landforms
Destructive plate margins

Destructive plate margins occur where two plates converge and one plate plunges under the other due to the movement of the **convection currents**. At this point the plate is re-incorporated into the upper mantle and crust. The area where this material is lost is called a **subduction zone**.

The three main types of destructive plate margin are as follows:

1 Oceanic/continental convergence: here, part of the ocean floor is dragged down by a downward gravitational force (known as **slab pull**) beneath a continental crust, with the sinking crust forming a very deep trench, parallel to the coast. An example is the Peru/Chile trench off the west coast of South America, where the Nazca and South American plates converge. In turn, the overriding South American Plate is being lifted up, creating a chain of **young fold mountains**, the Andes. The friction between the sinking oceanic plate and the continental plate creates great heat and melting, resulting in volcanoes along the length of the mountain chain. Strong, destructive earthquakes and the rapid uplift of mountain ranges are common in this region.

2 Oceanic/oceanic convergence (island arcs): when two oceanic plates converge, one usually sinks (subducts) under the other and in the process a trench is formed. For example, the Marianas Trench marks where the fast-moving Pacific Plate converges against the slower-moving Philippine Plate. Subduction processes in oceanic/oceanic plate convergence also result in the formation of volcanoes that, over millions of years, pile up lava on the ocean floor until a submarine volcano rises above sea level to form an island volcano. Such volcanoes are typically strung out in curved chains called **island arcs**. The descending plate also provides a source of stress as the two plates interact, leading to frequent moderate to strong earthquakes.

3 Continental/continental convergence: as the plates forming continental crust have a much lower density than the underlying layers, there is no subduction where they meet. Hence, as these plates move towards each other, their edges and the sediments between them are forced up to create fold mountains. There is no volcanic activity, but the movement of the plates can trigger shallow-focus earthquakes. Material can also be forced downwards to form deep mountain roots. An example of such a margin is where the Indo-Australian Plate is being forced northwards into the Eurasian Plate, creating the Himalayas.

Constructive plate margins

Constructive plate margins occur where two plates diverge away from each other, allowing new magma to reach the surface. There are examples of constructive plate margins on both sea and land. For the former, mid-ocean ridges are created, whereas for the latter, rift valleys occur.

An example of a mid-ocean ridge is the mid-Atlantic ridge (MAR). This is a submerged mountain range that runs north/south for 15,000 km through the Atlantic Ocean, from Iceland to a point 7,200 km east of southern South America. It breaks the ocean's surface in several places, forming groups of volcanic islands such as Iceland and Tristan da Cunha.

Destructive (or convergent) margins Where crust is destroyed as one plate dives under another.

Exam tip

Familiarise yourself with the names of volcanoes associated with each of these two types of convergence. A map showing the distribution of volcanoes will help.

Constructive (or divergent) margins Where new crust is generated as the plates pull away from each other.

The MAR is split by a deep rift valley along its crest, 10 km wide with walls 3,000 m high on either side. It marks the boundary between the two divergent plates of the ocean's floor. This rift valley is widening at a rate of 3 cm per year. Magma from beneath the Earth's surface rises to create the high ridges on either side, which, with further **gravitational sliding**, push away the lithosphere on either side (known as **ridge push**). This means that the rocks of the ocean floor on either side of the ridge move sideways, a process known as **sea-floor spreading**.

A rift valley system exists in East Africa where divergence has created the Great East African Rift system, which extends from the Red Sea in the north to the East African Highlands, Tanzania, in the south. These rifts are the site of some major lake basins, including lakes Malawi, Tanganyika and Edward. Individual rifts are tens of kilometres in length, up to 50 km wide and 1–5 km deep. Some geologists consider them to be incipient plate margins, and this is supported by the existence of volcanoes such as Mt Kilimanjaro.

Conservative plate margins

A conservative plate margin exists where two plates do not come directly into collision but slide past each other, in parallel, along a fault. The most well known example of such a boundary is the San Andreas Fault in California, USA, which separates the northward moving Pacific Plate (moving at 6 cm per year) and North American Plate (moving at 3 cm per year). This is a zone of intense earthquake activity, because the movement along the faults is irregular rather than a smooth process of gradual creep.

Magma plumes

The theory of plate tectonics offers an all-embracing explanation of the current distribution of the Earth's continents, volcanoes and earthquakes. There are, however, some exceptions.

For example, the Hawaiian Islands are a zone of great volcanoes and yet they do not occur at the boundary of a plate. While the vast majority of earthquakes and volcanic eruptions occur near plate margins, the Hawaiian Islands have formed in the middle of the Pacific Ocean, more than 3,200 km from the nearest plate boundary. The Hawaiian Island chain has resulted from the Pacific Plate moving over a deep, stationary hotspot in the mantle, located beneath the present-day position of the island of Hawaii (known as the 'Big Island'). Heat from this hotspot produces a constant source of magma by partially melting the overriding Pacific Plate. The magma, which is lighter than the surrounding solid rock, then rises through the mantle and crust (as a thermal **magma plume**) to erupt onto the sea floor. Over time, countless eruptions have caused a volcano to grow until it finally emerged above sea level to form an island. Continuing plate movement (from southeast to northwest) will eventually carry the island beyond the hotspot and volcanic activity will cease.

To the far northwest of the islands is a chain of underwater seamounts — the remnants of volcanic activity that took place even further back in time. This is further evidence that the plates on the Earth's crust are moving.

Knowledge check 4

Paleomagnetism provides evidence of sea-floor spreading. What is paleomagnetism, and how does it support the idea of sea-floor spreading?

Exam tip

Familiarise yourself with the names of volcanoes associated with constructive plate margins. A map showing the distribution of volcanoes will help.

Conservative (or transform) margins Where crust is neither produced nor destroyed as the plates slide horizontally past each other.

Hotspot Area in which heat under the Earth's crust is localised. At such points, rising magma can produce volcanoes.

Knowledge check 5

Some geologists suggest that Iceland sits on a hotspot. Investigate this theory.

Volcanic hazards

The nature of vulcanicity and its relation to plate tectonics

Volcanoes are built by the accumulation of their own eruptive products: lava, bombs (crusted-over ash deposits) and tephra (airborne ash and dust). A volcano is most commonly a conical hill or mountain built around a vent that connects with reservoirs of molten rock below the surface of the Earth. There are approximately 500 active volcanoes around the world. Only a few of them are erupting at any one time. An eruption is when a volcano gives off quantities of lava, ash or volcanic gas. A few volcanoes erupt more or less continuously (e.g. Mauna Loa, Hawaii), but others lie dormant between eruptions, when they give out very little gas and lava. The type of volcano and volcanic activity depends upon the nature of the lava. This in turn depends upon the location of the volcano with regard to tectonic plate margins. If the lava is a thin fluid (not viscous), then gases may escape easily. But if the lava is thick and dense (highly viscous) the gases will not move freely but will build up tremendous pressure, and ultimately escape with explosive eruptions (see Tables 2 and 3).

> **Vulcanicity** The process through which gases and molten rock are either extruded on the Earth's surface or intruded into the Earth's crust. It is clearly linked to the existence of plate margins.

Table 2 Variations in the type of volcanic activity in relation to plate margin type

	Destructive margin	Hotspot	Constructive margin
Magma source	A mix of old oceanic plate, ocean sediments and continental fragments, often weathered by water	Deep in the asthenosphere (mantle)	Deep in the asthenosphere (mantle)
Rock name	Andesite/Rhyolite	Basalt/Gabbro	Basalt/Gabbro
Magma chemistry	Medium to high acidity, greater than 63% SiO_2 (silica) content	Quite basic (alkaline), sometimes relatively rich in sodium and potassium, low silica content (around 50%)	Very basic (alkaline), low silica content, typically high iron and magnesium content
Magma's physical character	Viscous (solidifies quickly), flows over short distances, solidifies even on steep slopes, allows gases to build up pressure — can explode violently	Quite non-viscous (fairly runny), flows over low-angled slopes or can erupt as an ash	Very non-viscous (runny), flows long distances over very low-angled slopes or can create a black ash (tephra) when exploding with water vapour (steam)

Table 3 Variations in the type of volcanic activity in relation to lava type

	Basaltic lava	Andesitic lava	Rhyolitic lava
Silica content	45–50%	55–60%	65%
Eruption temperature	1,000°C+	800°C	700°C
Viscosity and gas content	Very runny, low gas	Sticky, intermediate gas	Very sticky, high gas
Volcanic products	Very hot, runny lava (shield volcanoes, low land or plateaux)	Sticky lava flows, tephra, ash, gas (composite volcanoes)	Pyroclastic flows, gas and volcanic ash (domes)
Eruption interval	Can be almost continuous, as on Hawaii	Decades or centuries	Millennia
Tectonic setting	Oceanic hotspots and constructive margins	Destructive plate margins (ocean/continental and ocean/ocean)	Continental hotspots and continental/continental margins
Processes	Dry partial melting of the upper mantle/lower lithosphere, basaltic magma is generally uncontaminated by water etc.	Wet partial melting of subducting oceanic crust contaminated by water and other material as magma rises	In situ melting of lower continental crust, most rhyolitic (granitic) magmas cool before they reach the surface
Hazardous?	Not really	Very	Very (but rare)

Form and impact of volcanic hazards

The impact of a volcanic event is only deemed hazardous when it has an effect on people. Figure 3 summarises the various forms of hazardous volcanic activity.

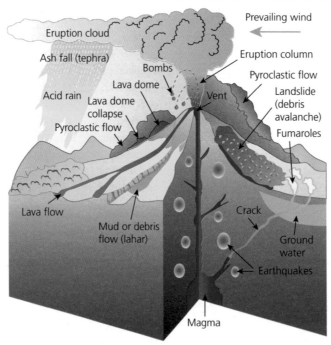

Figure 3 Forms of volcanic hazard

Exam tip

The forms of hazard associated with a volcano will vary according to the individual volcano studied. When examining your chosen case study of a recent volcanic event (see page 17), make sure you note the forms of hazard for that volcano.

A volcanic event can produce a number of hazardous effects, the impact of which can range from the area immediately around the volcano to the entire planet. They include the following:

- **Tephra:** solid material of varying grain size (from fine ash up to volcanic bombs) ejected into the atmosphere. Buildings often collapse under the sheer weight of ash falling onto their roofs. Air, thick with ash, is very difficult to breathe, and can cause serious respiratory problems. Fine tephra can also contribute to acid rain.
- **Pyroclastic flows:** very hot (800°C), gas-charged, high-velocity flows (over 200 km/h) of a mixture of gases and tephra. These flows devastate everything in their path.
- **Nuée ardente:** a glowing cloud of hot gas, steam and dust, volcanic ash and larger pyroclasts produced during a violent eruption, which can descend the slopes of a volcano at high velocity.
- **Lava flows:** at the speed at which most lava flows, it does not usually pose a threat to life. Lava flows do, however, represent a threat to farmland, property and infrastructure.
- **Volcanic gases:** these include carbon dioxide, carbon monoxide, hydrogen sulphide, sulphur dioxide and chlorine.
- **Lahars:** volcanic mudflows such as the one that devastated the Colombian town of Armero after the eruption of Nevado del Ruiz in November 1985, which buried some people alive.
- **Flooding:** caused by the melting of ice caps and glaciers, such as glacial bursts (or jökulhlaup).

Exam tip

Although you have to study one case study of a recent volcanic event in detail, be aware of the **impacts** of other volcanic events (although this doesn't require quite as much detail).

- **Tsunamis:** giant sea waves set off by huge explosions, such as the one that devastated the island of Krakatoa in 1883.
- **Climatic change:** the ejection of vast amounts of volcanic debris into the atmosphere can reduce global temperatures and is believed to have been an agent in past and present climatic change.

One way of classifying a volcano's hazardous nature is by its explosivity, using the Volcanic Explosivity Index (VEI). A volcano's impact can be judged in terms of its primary and secondary effects, and the environmental, social, economic and political consequences, both short and long term. Make sure you include these in your case study of a recent volcanic event (see below).

Management and responses

The management of and responses to volcanic events fall into two categories.

1 Prediction:
  - Study the eruption history of the volcano.
  - Measure gas emissions, land swelling, groundwater levels.
  - Measure the shock waves generated by magma travelling upwards.

2 Protection:
  - Assess the hazard, i.e. try to determine the areas of greatest risk that should influence land-use planning.
  - Dig trenches to divert the lava.
  - Build barriers to slow down lava flows.
  - Administer explosive activity to try to divert a lava flow.
  - Pour water on the lava front to slow it down.

Knowledge check 6

How can geologists determine the frequency of volcanic eruptions?

Exam tip

Although you have to study one case study of a recent volcanic event in detail, be aware of the **management of and responses to** other volcanic events (although this doesn't require quite as much detail).

Case study requirement

You are required to study **one recent volcanic event**, its impacts and the human responses to it. Possible volcanoes include: Mt St Helens (Washington, USA), Mt Nyiragongo (DRC), Mt Etna (Italy), Soufrière Hills volcano (Montserrat), Mt Merapi (Indonesia) and Eyjafjallajökull (Iceland). The following framework (see Table 4) may assist in this process. Note: an example of a completed table (for an earthquake) is provided on pages 20-21.

Table 4 Case study disaster framework

Case study				
Location/Date				
Geographical context (e.g. plate boundary(ies))				
Description of event	**Magnitude**	**Duration**	**Linked events**	**Other features**
Impacts	**Primary**		**Secondary**	
Environmental				
Social				
Economic				
Political				
Risk management including preparedness and prevention				
Mitigation strategies				
Adaptation strategies				

Seismic hazards

The nature of seismicity and its relation to plate tectonics

Most earthquakes occur along plate margins or deep under continents. Their location can also be linked to the distribution of certain geological characteristics, such as conservative plate margins and associated transform faults (low frequency but high predictability), ocean trenches and beneath fold mountains (greater frequency and high predictability).

As the Earth's crust is mobile, there can be a slow build-up of stress within the rocks where movement is taking place. When this stress is suddenly released, parts of the surface experience an intense shaking motion that lasts for just a few seconds. This is an earthquake. The depth of focus of an earthquake is significant:

- Shallow earthquakes (0–70 km) (75% of all energy released) cause the most damage.
- Intermediate (70–300 km) and deep (300–700 km) earthquakes have much less effect on the surface.

Earthquakes originate along faults. Parts of the crust are being forced to move in opposite directions, or in the same direction but at different speeds. These huge masses of rock get stuck, but the forces on them continue, building up stresses in the rocks. Eventually the strain overcomes the elastic strength of the rocks and they fracture, releasing large amounts of energy. At the moment of fracture the rocks regain their original shape but in a new position. The quaking and shaking takes place during the sudden movement of the rock back to its original shape, after the stress is released. This energy is transferred to the surrounding rocks, travelling through them as seismic waves. A lot of the energy is transferred vertically to the surface and then moves outwards from the epicentre.

Form and impact of seismic hazards

A seismic event is only deemed hazardous when it has an impact on people. It can produce a number of hazardous effects, the impact of which can range from the area close to the event to large parts of the planet. They include the following:

- **Earthquakes:** a series of vibrations and shock waves initiated by movements along the margins of tectonic plates.
- **Aftershocks:** smaller earthquakes that occur after a previous large earthquake in the same area.
- **Tsunamis:** large waves that flood areas along a coastline, often caused by submarine earthquakes. When they are out at sea, they have a very long wavelength, often in excess of 100 km. They are very short in amplitude, at around 1 m in height. They travel very quickly, often at speeds of up to 700 km/h, for example taking less than a day to cross the Pacific. When they reach land they rapidly increase in height, up to over 25 m in some cases. They are often preceded by a localised drop in sea level (drawback) as the approaching tsunami draws water back and up.

Exam tip

Although you are encouraged to keep up to date with events, when undertaking this case study it is recommended that you choose a disaster that has run its course and is at least 2/3 years old. In this way all of the requirements can be met.

Seismicity The geographic and historical distribution of earthquakes. Again, their distribution is closely associated with plate margins.

Focus The point below the Earth's surface at which an earthquake occurs.

Epicentre The point on the Earth's surface directly above the focus of an earthquake.

Exam tip

The forms of hazard associated with an earthquake will vary according to the individual earthquake studied. When examining your chosen case study of a recent seismic event (see pages 20–21), make sure you note the forms of hazard for that earthquake.

- **Liquefaction:** where soils with high water content lose their mechanical strength when shaken violently during an earthquake. They behave like a fluid.
- **Landslides:** mass movement of rock down a mountainside, triggered by the shaking of the ground during an earthquake.

An earthquake's magnitude is measured by a number of scales including (in order of date of development) the **Mercalli scale**, the **Richter scale** and the **moment magnitude scale (MMS)**. The Mercalli scale measures the effects of an earthquake and has a 12-point scale. The Richter scale measures the magnitude in terms of the energy released and has a 10-point logarithmic scale. Both of these have been superseded by the MMS (denoted as M_W), which also measures earthquakes in terms of the energy released. Humans rarely feel earthquakes of M_W2 or less. The scale is also logarithmic. An increase of 1 unit of magnitude increases the amount of shaking by 10, but the amount of energy released by 30.

A seismic hazard's impact can be judged in terms of its primary and secondary effects, and the environmental, social, economic and political consequences, both short and long term.

Management and responses

The management and responses to seismic events fall into three categories.

1 Prediction:
   - Study groundwater levels, the release of radon gas and animal behaviour.
   - Monitor fault lines and local magnetic fields.
   - Study fault lines to look for 'seismic gaps' at which the next earthquake may occur.

2 Prevention:
   - Keep the plates sliding past each other, rather than 'sticking' and then releasing. Suggestions include using water and/or oil.

3 Protection:
   - Build hazard-resistant (aseismic) structures. For example, install a large weight that can move with the aid of a computer program to counteract stress, have large rubber shock absorbers in foundations, have cross-bracing to hold the building when it shakes.
   - Retro-fit older buildings and elevated motorways with such devices.
   - Educate people in survival strategies and encourage earthquake drills.
   - Advise people in assembling earthquake kits, which include bottled water, canned food, clothing/bedding, a first aid kit, a torch, batteries, a can opener, matches and a small fire extinguisher.
   - Install 'smart' meters that cut off gas supplies at a certain tremor threshold.
   - Maintain organisation of emergency services, ensuring the correct gear is in place (such as that required for heavy lifting).
   - Plan land use to prevent certain buildings being constructed in high-risk areas.

Knowledge check 7

Explain how an earthquake causes a tsunami.

Exam tip

Although you have to study one case study of a recent seismic event in detail, be aware of the **impacts** of other seismic events (although this doesn't require quite as much detail).

Exam tip

Although you have to study one case study of a recent seismic event in detail, be aware of the **management of and responses to** other seismic events (although this doesn't require quite as much detail).

Case study requirement

You are required to study **one recent seismic event**, its impacts and the human responses to it. Possible earthquakes include: Northridge (Los Angeles, USA), Gujarat (India), the Boxing Day tsunami at Banda Aceh (Indonesia), L'Aquila (Italy), Tohoku (Japan), Haiti, Christchurch (New Zealand), Ghorka (Nepal) and Amatrice (Italy). A completed example is shown in Table 5.

Table 5 Case study framework: earthquakes example

Case study	The Sumatra–Andaman earthquake (Boxing Day tsunami)			
Location/Date	Epicentre off west coast of Sumatra/26 December 2004			
Geographical context	Occurred where the northward-moving (6 cm per year) Indo-Australian Plate subducts beneath the Burma Plate. There is an island arc (Andaman Islands) and a trench (Sunda Trench). Focus 30 km below the surface. There was a slip of 15 m along a 1,600 km fault.			
Description of event	**Magnitude**	**Duration**	**Linked events**	**Other features**
	9.1–$9.3\,M_W$	8–10 minutes	Indian Ocean tsunami	Daily aftershocks measuring up to $6.7\,M_W$ and lasting for 3 months
Impacts	**Primary**		**Secondary**	
Environmental	There was a 10 m movement laterally and 4–5 m vertically along the fault line. The seabed rose by several metres, which displaced $30\,km^3$ of water. This triggered a tsunami along the whole 1,600 km length of subduction. Banda Aceh province, the land mass closest to the epicentre of the earthquake, bore the full brunt. About 15 minutes after its eruption, the tsunami hit the west coast of Aceh. In some places, waves went inland 7.5 km from the coastline. Sri Lanka was the next worst affected because there was no other landmass between it and the epicentre. The waves hit over 2,260 km of coastline in the east and north of Sri Lanka. In many areas, the walls of water were up to 10 m high when they lashed against the shoreline. In some areas waves did not break, but continued inland as a fast stream of high water up to 5 km from the coast.		The smaller islands southwest of Sumatra have moved southwest by about 20 cm. Since movement was vertical as well as lateral, some coastal areas have been moved to below sea level. The Andaman and Nicobar Islands appear to have shifted southwest by around 1.25 m (and to have sunk by 1 m.) The earthquake had a huge effect on the topography of the seabed. 1,500 m high thrust ridges, created by previous geological activity along the fault, collapsed, generating submarine landslides several kilometres wide. One such landslide consisted of a single block of rock some 100 m high and 2 km long. The momentum of the water displaced by tectonic uplift also dragged massive slabs of rock, each weighing millions of tons, as far as 10 km across the seabed. An oceanic trench several kilometres wide was created in the seabed.	
Social	Indonesia was the worst affected area, with the death toll estimated to be as high as 220,000. Total casualties of 280,000 have been estimated. Eight people in South Africa died due to abnormally high sea levels and waves. Relief agencies reported that one-third of the dead were children. As many as four times more women than men were killed in some regions because they were waiting on the beach for the fishermen to return and looking after their children in the houses. Up to 9,000 tourists (mostly Europeans) were among the dead or missing. Sweden's death toll was 543.		1.8 million displaced people were spread over a dozen countries. There was significant loss of housing. Diseases spread, e.g. malaria, dengue fever, cholera and typhoid as well as 'Tsunami lung'. Cash-for-work programmes contributed to the reconstruction effort while providing jobs and prompting social development. Many women participating in such programmes received the same wages as men, for the first time.	

Economic	—	The total economic cost of damage was estimated at US$9.4 billion. In Aceh, the cost of damage (US$4.5 billion) was almost equal to the country's GDP in the previous year.
Political	Sri Lanka's civil war was halted temporarily as both sides helped in the rescue, recovery and the initial rebuilding phase following the tsunami.	Aceh had seen conflict between separatists and the government for 30 years. When the waves hit, fighting ceased as the parties became focused on the more immediate struggle for survival. In August 2005 a peace agreement was called for separatists to surrender their weapons and the government to withdraw its troops. This process was completed by December that year.
Risk management including preparedness and prevention	Despite a time lag of up to several hours between the earthquake and the impact of the tsunami in some parts of the Indian Ocean, nearly all of the victims were taken completely by surprise. There was no tsunami warning system in the Indian Ocean to warn the general population living around it. Tsunami detection is not easy because while a tsunami is in deep water, it has little height and a network of sensors is needed to detect it. Setting up the communications infrastructure to issue timely warnings is an even bigger problem, particularly in a relatively poor part of the world. There is a close connection between the magnitude of the damage the tsunami caused and poor coastal management. The high loss of life was partly a result of the destruction of natural defences, such as coral forests and mangrove swamps, and the building of oceanfront hotels and villas. For instance, the effects of the tsunami were less severe in areas along the east coast of Aceh, where the coastal ecosystem remained relatively untouched. In Sri Lanka the damage was very severe in coastal areas where there had been violation of regulations prohibiting the mining of coral reefs, and destruction of coastal mangrove forests, which act as buffers against high waves.	
Mitigation strategies	A tsunami warning system became active in June 2006, following the leadership of UNESCO. It consists of 25 seismographic stations and three deep-ocean sensors, which relay information to 26 national tsunami management centres.	
Adaptation strategies	The mobilisation of humanitarian aid (US$14 billion) was the largest ever international response to a natural disaster. The number of donor countries and humanitarian organisations involved were also far greater than in any previous natural disaster. Providing jobs such as rebuilding houses and weaving rope used in fishing nets has given income to farm workers who expected to miss a year's work due to the seawater inundation that rendered their farmland temporarily useless.	

Exam tip

Although you are encouraged to keep up to date with events, when undertaking this case study it is recommended that you choose a disaster that has run its course and is at least 2/3 years old. In this way all of the requirements can be met.

Storm hazards

The nature of tropical storms and their underlying causes

Tropical revolving storms are systems of intense low pressure (up to about 600–700 km across) formed over tropical sea areas. They move erratically until they reach land, where their energy is rapidly dissipated. At their centre is an area of subsiding air with calm conditions, clear skies and higher temperatures, known as the eye. In all cases they only become a true tropical revolving storm when the wind speed exceeds 120 km/h. Such storms are predictable in their spatial distribution. Hurricanes in the Caribbean are also predictable in their timing and frequency — usually towards the end of summer and into autumn. They are concentrated in the tropics, specifically between 5° and 20° north and south of the equator. Once generated they tend to move westwards initially, before then switching to a more northeastwards direction as they move further away from the equator.

Tropical revolving storms begin with an area of low pressure in the tropics into which warm air is drawn in a spiralling manner. Small-scale disturbances enlarge into tropical storms with rotating wind systems, which grow into a much more intense and rapidly rotating system. A number of factors largely determine this initial formation and subsequent transition:

- There must be an oceanic location where sea temperatures are over 27°C.
- The location must be at least 5° north or south of the equator so that the effect of the Coriolis force (CF) can bring about the maximum rotation of the air.
- Rapidly rising moist air (from the warm sea) cools and condenses, releasing latent heat energy, which then fuels the storm. Such storms fade and 'die' over land as the energy source is removed.
- Low-level convergence of air occurs in the lower part of the system, but this is then matched by intense upper atmosphere divergence of air, together creating an updraught of air.

Form and impact of storm hazards

The hazards associated with tropical storms include:

- high winds exceeding 150 km/h, which cause structural damage and collapse of buildings, damage to bridges and road infrastructure, and loss of agricultural land
- heavy rainfall, often over 100 mm a day, which causes river flooding and sometimes landslides, particularly in areas of high relief
- storm surges result from the piling up of water by wind-driven waves and the ocean rising up under reduced atmospheric pressure — such coastal flooding can extend inland if the area near the coast is flat and unprotected

The **magnitude** of tropical storms is measured on the Saffir–Simpson hurricane wind scale, which consists of five levels of central pressure, wind speed, storm surge and damage potential. The scale is summarised in Table 6.

Knowledge check 8

What are the various names of tropical storms around the world?

Coriolis force (CF) The effect of the Earth's rotation on air flow. In the northern hemisphere, the CF causes a deflection in the movement of air to the right, whereas in the southern hemisphere it is to the left.

Exam tip

The forms of hazard associated with a tropical storm will vary according to the individual storm studied. When examining your two chosen case studies of recent tropical storms (see below), make sure you note the forms of hazard for those storms.

Table 6 The Saffir–Simpson hurricane wind scale

Category of storm	Wind speed (km/h)	Effect	Storm surge (m above normal water levels)
1	120–153	■ No real damage to building structures ■ Some damage to trees and vegetation ■ Some risk of coastal flooding	1.2–1.5
2	154–178	■ Some roofing material, door and window damage ■ Considerable vegetation damage	1.6–2.4
3	179–209	■ Some structural damage to small houses and utility buildings ■ Extensive coastal flooding	2.5–3.6
4	210–249	■ Extensive damage ■ Complete roof collapses possible for small houses ■ Extensive coastal erosion and flooding extending well inland	3.7–5.5
5	250+	■ Complete roof failure on many dwellings and industrial buildings ■ Major flood damage ■ Massive evacuation of residential areas may be required	5.5+

A storm hazard's impact can be judged in terms of its primary and secondary effects, and the environmental, social, economic and political consequences, both short and long term.

Management and responses

A number of responses and risk management strategies exist in attempting to deal with tropical storms.

The management and responses to tropical storm events fall into several categories.

1 Prediction:
  - Predicting storms' origins and tracks — a form of **preparedness**. This depends on the quality of monitoring and warning systems. It is essential that warnings are as accurate as possible. Forecasting the precise power and track of a tropical storm remains problematic. The USA maintains round-the-clock surveillance of hurricanes using weather aircraft in order to increase its preparedness.

2 Prevention:
  - Ongoing research into how tropical storms can be tamed through **mitigation**. Much of this effort is directed at ways of reducing the storm's energy while it is still over the ocean. One attempt has been to 'seed' the storm using silver iodide outside of the eye-wall clouds. The idea is to produce rainfall, so releasing latent heat that would otherwise sustain the high wind speeds.
  - Better computer forecasting models. New technologies allow forecasters to break storms into a grid, and to use sophisticated methods to predict changes in wind speed, humidity, temperature and cloud cover. The National Oceanic and Atmospheric Administration (NOAA) in the USA has a high-resolution model to enable greater forecasting accuracy.
  - Schoolchildren in Florida practise hurricane drills, similar to those in earthquake-prone areas, as part of an awareness programme called Project Safeside.

Knowledge check 9

Why is it essential that storm warnings are accurate?

3 Protection:
- Land-use planning so that areas at highest risk have limited development, and therefore less potential economic damage.
- Strengthening of buildings to withstand storms and floods, or erecting houses/ buildings on stilts.
- Construction of seawalls, breakwaters and flood barriers.
- Adequate insurance before the disaster, and aid during and after the event, which contributes towards modifying any loss.

The impact of tropical storms depends on a range of political and economic factors. Areas with lower levels of economic development suffer from a lack of insurance, poor land-use planning, inadequate warning systems and defences, and poor infrastructure and emergency services. This usually results in a higher death toll. Even within a wealthy country such as the USA, Hurricane Katrina exposed the problems of a largely uninsured and relatively poor population who struggled to cope during, and especially after, the event.

Case study requirement

You are required to study **two recent tropical storms in contrasting areas** — their impacts and the human responses to them. Possible storms include: Cyclone Nargis (Myanmar), Hurricane Katrina (USA), Typhoon Haiyan (Philippines), Hurricane Sandy and Hurricane Matthew (both the Caribbean and the USA). Use a table similar to that on page 17 for each tropical storm event.

Fires in nature

The nature of wildfires and their underlying causes

Wildfires, commonly known as bushfires (Australia) or brush fires (USA/Canada), are a normal occurrence in many ecosystems. We must first distinguish between managed fires and wildfires. **Managed fires** are frequently used in conservation areas such as wildernesses (for example New South Wales) and remote national parks (for example Yellowstone) as a necessary and beneficial tool of ecosystem management.

In contrast, **wildfires** are human-induced fires that have got out of control and can no longer be classed as managed, or have been deliberately started with malicious intent or through carelessness. Many wildfires occur naturally as a result of lightning strikes, although it is estimated that lightning causes only 10% of wildfires.

The nature, intensity and rate of spread of a wildfire depend on the types of plants involved, the topography, the strength and direction of the winds, and the relative humidity of the air in the region. Some fires travel close to the ground, others spread via the canopies of tall trees. Wildfires are particularly associated with areas experiencing semi-arid climates where there is enough rainfall for vegetation to grow and provide a 'fuel', yet with a dry season to promote conditions for ignition.

Exam tip

Although you are encouraged to keep up to date with events, when undertaking this case study it is recommended that you choose a disaster that has run its course and is at least 2/3 years old. In this way all of the requirements can be met.

Knowledge check 10

Why are managed fires used in some areas?

Wildfires are therefore concentrated in parts of Australia (New South Wales and Victoria), Canada (British Columbia), the USA (California and Florida), South Africa and southern Europe (Mediterranean areas). Some geographers have suggested that such fires have become more prevalent in these areas as there is more movement of people into the countryside, as well as an increased incidence of drought due to climate change.

Traditionally, wildfires have not been associated with areas of tropical rainforest because of the high humidity and all year round rainfall. However, the burning of the rainforest in Indonesia, for example for clearance and forest mismanagement by logging companies, combined with the drying effect of El Niño events, have revised this view. Indeed, the combination of drying winds and the burning of relatively moist timber has led to particularly smoky wildfire-related events in parts of southeast Asia in recent years. Toxic hazes from such fires, combined with other forms of air pollution, have been an increasingly common phenomenon in cities such as Kuala Lumpur and Singapore.

Impacts of wildfires

The impacts of wildfires include:
- loss of timber, livestock and crops
- loss of valuable plant species and the creation of areas dominated by fire-resistant scrub
- damage to soil structure and nutrient content, which occurs over a wide area
- loss of wildlife, of particular concern when rare or endemic species are involved
- in the case of extensive fires, loss of vegetation leading to an increased risk of flooding
- temporary evacuation usually requiring emergency aid for the areas affected
- property loss increasing as a result of settlement expansion into at-risk areas
- release of toxic gases and particulate pollution
- risk to firefighters (although loss of life in general is quite low)
- heavy impact on emergency services (huge costs and large numbers of people involved in controlling the outbreak)

The impact of a wildfire can be judged in terms of the fire's primary and secondary effects, and the environmental, social, economic and political consequences, both short and long term.

Management and responses

A number of responses and risk management strategies exist in attempting to deal with wildfires.

1 Prevention:
   - In many countries such as Australia, Greece and Spain, the main approach to fire management has been to extinguish all fires as they occur, especially in populated areas or near to high-value timber reserves (mitigation). Management to modify wildfires also concentrates on reducing or eliminating the fuel supplies from the potential path of the fire by controlled burning. This practice is not only controversial, but also risky.

Knowledge check 11

Some plants are pyrophytic. What does this mean, and can you give examples?

Exam tip

The precise impact of a wildfire will vary according to the individual fire studied. When examining your chosen case study of recent wildfire event, make sure you note the **impact** of that event.

– Technology to warn areas at risk. Aircraft and satellites are used to carry out infrared sensing to check surface ground temperatures and signs of eco-stress from desiccation.

2 Protection:

– Community preparedness leading to early warning through the use of fire towers. Citizens can be trained to act as auxiliary firefighters, to organise evacuation and coordinate emergency firefighting.

– Education concerning home safety in high-risk areas. Supplies of fuel should be reduced, wood stores stacked correctly, and adequate water hose and ladders should be made available. Householders are also advised to remove dead leaves from gutters. School education concentrates on ensuring young people understand the dangers of arson and casual cigarette use, and the need to adhere to barbeque laws in at-risk areas.

– Land-use planning (adaptation). Risk management identifies areas of high vulnerability, and planning legislation ensures houses are built in low-density clusters with at least 30 m set back from any forested area. New developments can be designed with fire breaks and wide roads to allow access for firefighting equipment.

– Fire-resistant housing design is increasingly important in at-risk areas.

– Insurance is another option, although expensive and difficult to obtain in fire-prone areas.

> **Exam tip**
>
> Although you have to study one case study of a recent wildfire event in detail, be aware of the **management of and responses to** other wildfire events (although this doesn't require quite as much detail).

> **Exam tip**
>
> Although you are encouraged to keep up to date with events, when undertaking this case study it is recommended that you choose a disaster that has run its course and is at least 2/3 years old. In this way all of the requirements can be met.

Case study requirement

You are required to study **one recent wildfire event**, its impacts and the human responses to it. Possible wildfires include: southern Australia (2009), Indonesia (2014/15) and southern California, USA (2015/16). Use a table similar to that on page 17.

Further case study requirements

You are required to study **one multi-hazardous environment beyond the UK** to illustrate and analyse the nature of the hazards and the social, economic and environmental risks presented, and how human qualities and responses such as resilience, adaptation, mitigation and management contribute to its continuing human occupation.

Many of the rapidly growing mega-cities of the developed and developing world are located in hazard-prone areas and are possible areas for study. In some cases, rapid urbanisation has destroyed ecosystems through deforestation, which increases the risk of flash floods. Several such cities are in close proximity to plate margins and the tracks of tropical storms, and within dry but forested environments. Some are at risk of a combination of these hazards. With high population densities, hazard management in large urban areas is both expensive and complex, making disasters inevitable both socially (high concentrations of vulnerable people) and economically (huge investment in infrastructure). Such urban areas include Los Angeles, Tokyo, Bangkok, Manila and Calcutta.

You are also required to study **a specified place (at a local scale) in a hazardous setting** to illustrate the physical nature of the hazard, and analyse how the economic, social and political character of its community reflects the presence and impacts of the hazard, and the community's response to the risk.

You could choose to study another case study of an area affected by a volcano or an earthquake or a tropical storm. However, you might want to consider making use of one of your earlier case studies — just make sure it is at a relatively smaller scale. An individual affected city would satisfy this requirement — Kobe (Japan), Christchurch (New Zealand) or New Orleans (USA) would be ideal.

Summary

After studying this topic, you should be able to:

- understand the concept of a hazard in a geographical context and appreciate the variety of forms, impacts and responses that exist in the study of hazards. On the other hand, a model of hazard management for all has been developed
- know and understand the theory of plate tectonics, and understand how it and associated processes explain the formation and characteristics of a variety of landforms
- explain how volcanic hazards are created, and be able to discuss their impacts and the variety of responses to them, with particular emphasis on one case study
- explain how seismic hazards are created, and be able to discuss their impacts and the variety of responses to them, with particular emphasis on one case study
- explain how tropical storm hazards are created, and be able to discuss their impacts and the variety of responses to them, with particular emphasis on two case studies
- explain how wildfire hazards are created, and be able to discuss their impacts and the variety of responses to them, with particular emphasis on one case study
- understand how some areas of the world suffer from a combination of hazards, and recognise that a range of managements strategies are therefore required in those areas

Population and the environment

Introduction

The environmental context for human population characteristics and change

Population is unevenly distributed over space, both at a global scale and at a national scale. A number of key physical environmental elements provide reasons for this (see Tables 7 and 8).

Table 7 Environmental elements affecting sparsely populated areas

Environmental element	Sparsely populated areas
Relief	- Rugged mountains where temperatures are low (the Andes, the Himalayas) - Active volcanic areas (Iceland)
Climate	- Areas of very low annual rainfall (Sahara desert) - Areas of long seasonal drought (the Sahel) - Areas with high humidity (the Amazon) - Very cold areas (northern Canada, Siberia)
Vegetation	- The coniferous forests of northern Eurasia and northern Canada - The rainforests of the Amazon and Zaire basins
Soils	- The frozen soils (permafrost) of the Arctic and Siberia - The thin soils of mountainous areas - The leached soils of the Amazon rainforest where forest clearance has occurred - The overgrazed areas of the Sahel
Resources	- Areas lacking in fuel resources and valuable mineral resources - The areas where extensive farming takes place
Water supplies	- Areas lacking a permanent supply of fresh clean water due to irregular rainfall, or few wells and reservoirs (Sudan and Ethiopia)

Table 8 Environmental elements affecting densely populated areas

Environmental element	Densely populated areas
Relief	■ Flat lowland areas (The Netherlands and Bangladesh) ■ Relatively stable and fertile volcanic areas (Mt Etna)
Climate	■ Areas with reliable, evenly distributed rainfall, a lengthy growing season, no temperature extremes (western Europe) ■ Areas with high levels of sunshine (California)
Vegetation	■ Areas of grassland, which encourage pastoral farming that supports relatively dense populations (Denmark, Pampas of Argentina)
Soils	■ Areas with deep, rich in humus soils such as those found in alluvial river basins (the Ganges valley, Paris area, the Nile delta) and which support intensive farming
Resources	■ Areas with extensive deposits of coal close to the surface (Rhine-Ruhr, Donbas, Yorkshire/Lancashire) ■ Areas where intensive farming takes place (Ganges valley, the Low Countries, east coast of China)
Water supplies	■ Areas with a regular and reliable supply of water. These may be areas with an evenly distributed rainfall (northwest Europe) or heavy seasonal rainfall (the monsoon lands of southeast Asia)

Exam tip

Be prepared to make comparative points based on Tables 7 and 8. For example, illustrate the role of resources and water supplies in determining sparsely and densely populated areas.

Key population parameters

Population parameters concern the distribution and density of a population, as well as the sheer **numbers** involved and rates of change. **Population change** is examined in more detail later (see page 42).

Population distribution is usually displayed by a dot map. Areas that have a large number of people per unit area are densely populated. Areas that have few people per unit area are sparsely populated.

The population density of a country or region is obtained by dividing the total population of that country or region by its total area. This, however, can be misleading as it does not show the variations between densely populated areas and those that are almost unpopulated. Population density is usually displayed by a choropleth, or shading map.

In terms of the number of people, in the summer of 2016, the world's population stood at 7.5 billion. Over 6 billion of these lived in developing countries, with 1.3 billion living in developed countries. Half of the world's population live in just six countries: China, India, the USA, Indonesia, Brazil and Pakistan. Demographers suggest that by 2043 the global population will reach 9 billion.

Nearly half of the world's population (some 3 billion) is under the age of 25, and there are 1.2 billion between the ages of 15 and 24. These people are entering their child-rearing years. Their attitudes and responses to birth control will determine whether or not the world reaches 11 billion by 2100. The world's youngest countries (i.e. those with the highest proportions under 15 years old) are all in Africa.

Population distribution Its spatial occurrence, i.e. where people are located and where they are not.

Population density The number of people per unit area, for example per km^2.

Knowledge check 12

What determines the number of people that can live on the planet?

The key role of development processes

Development processes have been manifested in key moments of the history of the planet from the agrarian revolution of Stone Age times to the Industrial Revolution that began in the UK in the 18th century. Closer to the present, we have seen the Green Revolution of the 1960s, when new hybrid seeds were introduced, and the technological revolution of the 21st century. Development processes have involved the production of more food, industrial development and even the control of many of the threats to population — diseases and pests, for example. Development processes have enabled more people to live on the planet.

It is suggested that a youthful population provides an opportunity for a country to capitalise on its youthfulness and thereby stimulate economic growth — a so-called **demographic dividend** (see page 44). This would be a continuation of the process of development over time, whereby ever-growing numbers of people have made use of the resources available to them in order to improve their living standards.

Global patterns of population numbers, densities and change rates

References to these have been made earlier, and they are constantly being updated. You are advised to study online data such as the World Population Data Sheet produced by the Population Reference Bureau (www.prb.org/) to keep up to date with global patterns of population numbers, densities and rates of change.

Various world population clocks, such as www.census.gov/popclock/, are also useful.

Environment and population

Patterns of food production and consumption

World food production continues to increase, yet the rate at which it is increasing has slowed. Equally, the world has made significant progress in raising food consumption per capita. In general terms the growth in food consumption has been accompanied by a change in diet, away from staples such as roots and tubers towards more livestock products and vegetable oils.

Some points about food production and consumption follow.
- Much food is produced and consumed locally (especially in poorer countries) or, in the case of richer countries, it is produced within the same country of consumption.
- An increasing proportion of food is produced not for domestic markets but for sale in the world's markets. Specialisation and the commercialisation of agriculture drive this change.
- The actions of transnational corporations (TNCs), and the need for governments of developing countries to raise income through export earnings, have led to the export of many crops from poorer nations, even if there are local food shortages in those countries.
- Food travels increasingly long distances (measured by food miles), as technological advances in air, sea and freight take place, together with improvements in storage techniques, which ensure food stays fresh.

Demographic dividend
The benefit a country gets when its working population is much larger than its dependent population (children and the retired).

Knowledge check 13

How can a 'demographic dividend' become a 'demographic debt' as a country develops?

- Demand for non-seasonal foodstuffs in richer nations is high (e.g. in winter, strawberries are flown from Chile to the UK).
- Many countries are net importers of food. Many countries in this situation are in sub-Saharan Africa, where undernourishment is rife, but this is also the case in the UK.
- Few countries are net exporters of food and these countries have few undernourished people (e.g. USA, Canada, Australia, New Zealand and Argentina).
- Agricultural exports can make up a large percentage of poorer countries' export earnings, but generally form only a very small percentage of developed country export earnings.

There are clear patterns of food consumption. The richest nations consume the most kilocalories per day (between 2,600 up to 3,800), including those in North America and Europe, Australia, South Korea, Japan and parts of South America. Large parts of Central Africa, Asia and South America consume far fewer calories and here many people can be said to be suffering from undernutrition — where people consume less than the WHO's recommended daily minimum totals of 1,940 kcal for women and 2,550 kcal for men.

An added problem for those countries in which people suffer undernutrition is that of malnutrition. This is where people may get sufficient calories a day but not have a balanced diet — much of their calorie intake might come just from rice.

Agricultural systems and productivity

Farms can be considered as open systems (see Figure 4). The inputs include physical, cultural, economic and behavioural influences. Generally, as an area develops economically, the physical factors become less important as the human inputs increase in influence.

> **Exam tip**
>
> Examiners are likely to provide world maps for this area of study. Make sure you check which show production and which show consumption.

> **Exam tip**
>
> As with any system, examine the feedback mechanisms, both positive and negative.

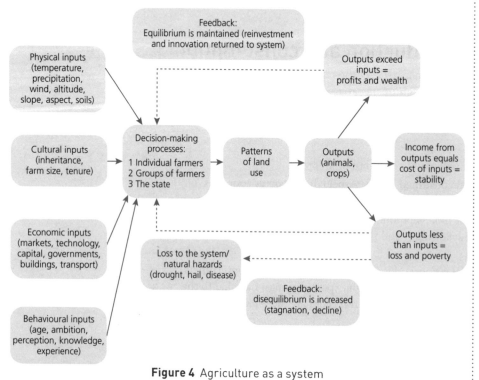

Figure 4 Agriculture as a system

There are several systems of farming that have differing levels of agricultural productivity.

- **Intensive farming** is usually relatively small scale and can either be:
  - capital intensive, i.e. money is invested in soil improvement, machinery, buildings, pest control and high quality seeds/animals. There are few people employed and so output is high per hectare and per worker, for example market gardening in the Netherlands.
  - labour intensive, i.e. the number of farm workers is high and so there is a high output per hectare but a low output per worker, for example rice cultivation in the Ganges valley of India.
- **Extensive farming** is carried out on a large scale over a large area. This varies greatly. There are areas in which, although the labour force is low, there is a high capital input, for example on high-quality seeds/animals or pesticides and insecticides, such as wheat farming in the Canadian Prairies. Other areas still have a low labour force but rely on the sheer amount of land they are farming to provide sufficient output for their needs, for example sheep ranching in Australia.

So, agricultural systems can be a combination of:

- commercial or subsistence
- intensive or extensive
- arable (crops), livestock (animals) or mixed.

Some forms of agriculture are so affected by human influences that they can be regarded as being highly specialised. This can range from high intensities of one crop (monoculture) to highly technological forms such as hydroponics, where soils are deemed to be unnecessary.

Commercial farming
Where the outputs (crops, animals) are sold.

Subsistence farming
Where the outputs are largely for consumption by the farmer with little or no surplus.

Relationships between climate, soils and agriculture

Despite the fact that human factors such as technological inputs are increasingly influential in agriculture, the key physical/environmental variables of climate and soils are still important for agriculture on a large scale. In simple terms, some places in the world are more suited for agriculture than others.

You are required to study **two major climatic types** to exemplify relationships between climate and human activities and numbers. You are also required to study the characteristics and distribution of **two key zonal soils** to exemplify the relationship between soils and human activities, especially agriculture. It is easier to combine these in two specific areas of study.

The following section examines **one area** where climate and soils are ideally suited to agriculture and food production, and hence have an influence on population numbers: the temperate grasslands of the Canadian prairies.

Exam tip

You should undertake a similar study of another area yourself, such as the monsoon areas of India and Bangladesh, or the Mediterranean coast of Europe.

The Canadian Prairies

In the mid-latitude continental interior of North America there are extensive areas of natural grassland. Much of this grassland has, in the last two centuries, been heavily modified by human activity and in particular by farming. People have ploughed up large areas for extensive wheat farming, and they used the rest for equally extensive cattle and sheep ranching. The natural relationship between climate and soils has greatly influenced the type of agriculture being undertaken here. Due to the nature of the agricultural activity, both the numbers and density of people are low.

Climatically, the conditions are as follows.
- The hottest months have temperatures between 27°C and 21°C, depending on latitude.
- The coolest months have temperatures between 0°C and –4°C.
- The annual range, therefore, is approximately 28–22°C.
- Rainfall totals are usually less than 500mm, with a summer maximum and some snow in winter.

The soils in this region are known as chernozems, or black earths. They are largely developed on vast expanses of wind-blown (aeolian) silts known as loess. These silts were laid down on the edges of the huge Pleistocene ice sheets at the end of the ice ages, and were blown there from the northern areas of moraine and outwash plains. These soils are ideal for the natural growth of grassland. Grass growth is vigorous in the spring and early summer, but the dry period in late summer and the frosts of winter slow down the natural processes of decomposition. Consequently, losses of organic material are reduced. The loess parent material also provides a source of calcium carbonate. There is a rich soil fauna, including various burrowing animals, which cause some mixing of the soil profile. Taking these factors together then, the surface layers of the soil are deep and humus-enriched, fertile and ideal for these forms of agriculture.

There is some debate as to whether the grasslands of the Prairies are entirely a natural response to climate and soils, or whether over time they have developed due to human activity, and are in fact a **plagioclimax**. Botanists have tended to believe that, under the prevailing conditions of climate and soil, the presence of a dense grass sod prevented the invasion and establishment of trees. High evapotranspiration rates were thought to give a competitive advantage to herbaceous plants with shallow, but dense, root systems. Overall, the land, climate and soils are ideal for the farming of grains and meat.

Plagioclimax Where human interference has permanently arrested and altered the natural vegetation of an area.

Knowledge check 14

What could be another reason for the lack of trees in the Canadian Prairies?

Climate change as it affects agriculture

Scientists state that climate change will have significant adverse effects on crop yields, livestock health and tree growth due to higher temperatures, extended heat waves, flooding, shifting precipitation patterns, and spreading habitats for pests (such as flies and mosquitoes) and diseases (such as wheat and coffee rusts). These will arise from relatively small increases in heat and humidity. Without adaptation, yields of the main cereals in developing countries are expected to be 10% lower by 2050 than they would have been without climate change. Water stress on cropping activity is also likely to increase due to growing water scarcity.

Studies suggest that the primary impact of climate change will be on the poor in tropical countries, mainly through decreased local food supply and higher food prices. The most significant effects are projected for Africa and South Asia, where poverty is highest. Here agriculture accounts for a large share of employment and GDP, and adaptation investment per capita is low. In general terms, the lower the capacity of people to adapt to climate change, the larger the negative impacts will be.

In 2012, the Food and Agriculture Organization (FAO) introduced the concept of climate-smart agriculture (CSA). The aim of this was to address both food insecurity and climate change, but the stated outcomes were extremely general:

- Agricultural productivity should be increased in a sustainable fashion.
- Resilience to climate change should be enhanced.
- Agriculture should do its bit to reduce greenhouse gas emissions.

Knowledge check 15

Give some specific forms of climate-smart agriculture (CSA).

Soil problems

Human activity is capable of having a massive impact upon soils. It can either damage them (degradation) or improve the situation (upgrade). The degradation of soils is the result of human failure to understand and manage the resource.

Soil erosion

Soil erosion is most rapid in those areas where there is the misuse of the land by people. Some activities that cause soil erosion are:

- the removal of vegetation by either chopping down trees or overgrazing by animals. In both cases the soil is exposed to the wind and the rain.
- the ploughing of land in the same direction as the slope. This encourages rilling to take place.

Soil erosion The washing away or blowing away of topsoil such that the fertility of the remaining soil is greatly reduced.

Gleying

Gleying is a process of soil formation that takes place when conditions are waterlogged, or anaerobic. Under such conditions the pore spaces are filled with stagnant water, which becomes de-oxygenised, causing the reddish-coloured oxidised iron (ferric) deposits in the soil to be chemically reduced to the blue-grey ferrous iron. Re-oxygenising causes red-orange patches to appear within the blue-grey soil, this process being known as mottling. Many of the soils of the upland UK show evidence of gleying.

Waterlogging Describes the state of a soil when all the pore spaces below a certain depth, known as the water table, are full of water.

Salinisation

Salinisation is a feature of areas with an arid or semi-arid climate. As moisture is evaporated from the surface, water containing salts is drawn upwards by capillary action. Further evaporation causes the deposition of the salts on the ground surface. The roots of plants that cannot tolerate saline conditions become affected and the plants die.

Salinisation Occurs when potential evapotranspiration is greater than precipitation and when the water table is near to the ground surface.

Structural deterioration

Soil structure refers to the manner in which individual particles of soil aggregate together. These aggregates are called peds, and they are stuck together by organic matter, and the secretions and mucilages from soil fauna. It is the shape and alignment of the peds that determine the size and number of pore spaces through which water, air and roots can penetrate. Therefore, they influence the agricultural value of the soil.

Examples of structural deterioration include the following:

- Over-cultivation of the soil by growing the same crop in the same field year after year (monoculture).
- The compaction of the soil by the use of heavy machinery or the trampling effect of animals. This reduces the rate of infiltration into the soil — water flows across its surface and therefore erodes it.

Knowledge check 16

Why has salinisation become a major problem in some irrigated areas?

Structural deterioration Occurs when human activity damages the basic structure of a soil.

Soil management and improvement

Badly soil-degraded areas can be managed and improved in a number of ways:

- Adding fertiliser improves nutrient content. This can be either inorganic (NPK fertilisers, which are compounds of nitrogen, phosphorous and potassium) or organic (mainly farmyard manure and crop residues). Organic fertilisers encourage soil organisms and improve nutrient retention. Artificial fertilisers do not do this, and there is concern about their impact on the environment (e.g. eutrophication of lakes and rivers).
- Planting crops or trees (afforestation) helps to stabilise the soil, and organic matter is returned to the soil through leaf litter.

Various farming practices can also improve the soil, including:

- crop rotation with fallow periods, allowing soil to replenish nutrients
- replacing hedgerows to reduce wind erosion
- improving field drainage to increase aeration
- ploughing across slopes to prevent gullying
- liming, providing more nutrients for plant growth and organism development
- mulching, for example by ploughing in the stubble, increases the organic content and improves nutrient retention

> **Exam tip**
>
> When considering a form of soil degradation be aware of the environmental conditions under which the process is operating.

Strategies to ensure food security

The World Food Summit of 1996 defined **food security** as existing 'when all people at all times have access to sufficient, safe, nutritious food to maintain a healthy and active life'. It can also be defined as including both physical and economic access to food that meets people's dietary needs as well as their food preferences.

With the global population expected to grow by 1.2 billion by 2030, and the proportion of 'middle class' people, who have higher expectations, set to double by 2030, pressures on food supplies are set to increase. According to the World Bank, 1.2 billion people still live on less than US$1.25 a day, and more than 800 million people go hungry every day. These people have low levels of food security or, put the other way, high levels of food insecurity.

To ensure food security globally, there have been several strategies adopted. These include the following:

The Green Revolution

This was a movement in the 1960s to increase crop yields by using new high-yielding varieties (HYVs) that had been developed. Through the use of irrigation, fertilisers, pesticides and mechanisation, they produced high yields per hectare.

The Green Revolution has been most successfully applied in Asia, where nine-tenths of all wheat and two-thirds of rice is produced using HYVs.

However, there are many disadvantages with the Green Revolution, including the following:

- Costly inputs of fertilisers and pesticides have led some farmers into debt.
- HYVs require more weed control.
- Mechanisation has led to rural unemployment and rural-urban migration.

Genetic modification (GM) of crops and animals

Genetic modification entails taking genes (a unit of heredity) from one species and adding them to the DNA (the genetic instructions used in the development and functioning of all known living organisms) of another species. The resultant plant or animal will have some of the better characteristics of the donor plant or animal in the resultant offspring.

Advantages of GM

There are several advantages to GM crops:
- Farmers can grow more, because it is easier to fight pests.
- Farmers also use less crop spray (which itself can also be environmentally friendly).

Disadvantages of GM

There are also several disadvantages to GM crops:
- Genes from the GM crop could be transferred to pests. The pests then become resistant to the crop spray.
- Plants can also pollinate weeds, which could then acquire pesticide resistance.

Other approaches

There are several other strategies and approaches employed in trying to maintain food security. These include the following:
- **Cloning:** cloning is used in agriculture to produce an identical reproduction of a strong and healthy crop.
- **Land colonisation:** in some developing countries, such as Brazil, government land policies encourage poor farmers to settle on forest lands. Each settler acquires the right to continue using a piece of land by living on a plot of unclaimed public land (no matter how marginal the land) and using it for at least 1 year and a day.
- **Land reform:** This generally entails the transfer of ownership of land from large (often absent) landowners to smaller resident farmers. Ownership tends to encourage farmers to invest in the land. Examples of land reform can be found in Bolivia, Brazil and India.
- **Appropriate/intermediate technology solutions:** In developing countries, high-tech solutions are not always suitable to the local conditions. Scientists have developed appropriate technology which poorly educated farmers can learn to use, thus becoming self-sufficient.

> **Knowledge check 17**
> Give two examples of the use of appropriate technology in agriculture.

Environment, health and wellbeing

Global patterns of health, mortality and morbidity

Mortality

Mortality in children under 5 years of age around the world declined by almost 60% between 1990 and 2015, from an estimated rate of 90 deaths per 1,000 live births to 37 deaths per 1,000 live births. This translates to over 18,000 fewer children dying

> **Mortality** State of being mortal or susceptible to death. There are various indicators of death, including crude death rate, infant mortality and maternal mortality.

every day in 2015 than in 1990. The risk of a child dying before their fifth birthday is still highest in the World Health Organization (WHO) African Region (59 per 1,000 live births) — ten times higher than that in the WHO European Region (6 per 1,000 live births). Nevertheless, nearly 19,000 children worldwide died every day in 2015, and the global speed of decline in mortality rate is disappointingly slow.

Morbidity

Morbidity is measured using the **disability-adjusted life year (DALY)**. This is a measure of overall disease burden, expressed as the number of years lost due to ill health, disability or early death. Originally developed by the WHO, it extends the concept of potential years of life lost due to premature death to include equivalent years of 'healthy' life lost by virtue of being in a state of either poor health or disability. Most morbidity can be attributed to disease, both infectious and non-communicable.

Infectious diseases include the most serious diseases, such as influenza, AIDS, malaria, cholera and yellow fever. However, morbidity does not just arise from infectious diseases. It also arises from non-communicable diseases (NCDs), such as cardiovascular diseases, cancers, chronic respiratory diseases and diabetes.

> **Exam tip**
>
> The WHO provides useful factsheets on NCDs in the world at www.who.int/mediacentre/factsheets/fs355/en/.

The epidemiological transition

In 1971, Omran put forward a model relating to population, health and disease — the Epidemiological Transition model. It states that societies undergo three 'ages' of health.

1 **An age of pestilence and famine:** a period in which mortality is high, with the principle causes of death being infectious diseases and poor maternal conditions, reinforced by nutritional deficiencies.

2 **An age of receding pandemics:** socio-economic developments and advances in medical science and healthcare mean infectious diseases are reduced and life expectancy increases. Examples of such improvements and advances include better public water supplies and the discovery of penicillin.

3 **An age of degenerative diseases:** as infectious diseases are controlled and people live longer, there is an increased visibility of degenerative diseases (cancers, heart disease). Diseases associated with modernisation and industrialisation (obesity, diabetes) increase.

Some writers have added a fourth stage — an age of delayed degenerative diseases. Here the causes of death are generally the same as the third stage (although dementia is more prevalent), but they occur later in the life cycle as life expectancy increases.

Omran stated that socio-economic development is responsible for the movement of a society through these 'ages'. As a model, the Epidemiological Transition model parallels the Demographic Transition Model (see page 43), from high fertility and

> **Exam tip**
>
> The World Population Data Sheet produced by the Population Reference Bureau (www.prb.org/) enables you to keep up to date with global patterns of mortality.

Morbidity Illness. It includes any diseased state, disability or condition of poor health.

mortality rates, with young populations with high levels of infectious disease, to societies with low fertility and mortality rates and ageing populations where NCDs predominate. For the latter to occur, a medical and healthcare revolution has to take place, which tackles and/or controls infectious diseases. The model therefore provides us with a useful reference point for exploring the linkages between health and socio-economic development.

Exam tip

Make sure you understand the terms 'infectious', 'non-communicable' and 'degenerative' when classifying diseases.

The relationship between environment variables and the incidence of disease

Several writers have sought to examine links between the natural environment and the incidence of disease. For example, there appear to be links between the medical conditions of asthma and hay fever and the prevalence of pollen and dust during warmer times, certainly in the UK.

There also appears to be a direct link with some aspects of the physical environment with the incidence of malaria. Malaria is a tropical disease, associated with a tropical climate. However, it has also been endemic in other parts of the world in the past, for example in Mediterranean Europe. The key is the existence of a particular form of mosquito, which spreads the malaria parasite. Mosquitoes breed in warm areas of stagnant water, and hence are common in flat lowland marshy areas.

In recent years another tropical disease — Ebola — has featured strongly in the news. Is this also a function of the natural environment (another hot environment) or is its spread more complicated? Between 1976 and 2014, the disease was confined to a narrow equatorial climatic belt between southern Sudan and Uganda, west through the Democratic Republic of Congo (DRC) to Gabon, Liberia, Sierra Leone and Guinea. However some factors that contributed to the Ebola epidemic are deeply rooted in local cultural practices. Bodies are extremely infectious just after death, but local funeral rituals include someone, often a family member, washing and re-dressing the body prior to burial. People have strongly held beliefs that bad luck, or ill-health, will befall a family that does not carry out funeral rites in a traditional, respectful way. This is not an environmental link.

A further factor is the widespread consumption of bush meat from the local environment in rural Africa. Although not fully proven, fruit bats are suspected to be a natural wild host of Ebola. Such creatures only exist in the tropical environmental conditions — both climatic and ecological — that allow them to flourish.

Deterministic links between environment and disease are therefore far from clear.

Air quality and health

Air pollution is a major environmental risk to health. By reducing air pollution levels, countries can reduce the burden of disease from stroke, heart disease, lung cancer and both chronic and acute respiratory diseases, including asthma. The lower the levels of air pollution, the better the cardiovascular and respiratory health of the population will be, both in the long and short term.

According to the WHO, ambient (outdoor air) pollution, in both cities and rural areas, was estimated to cause 3.7 million premature deaths worldwide in 2013. Some 88%

of those premature deaths occurred in low- and middle-income countries, with the greatest number in the WHO Western Pacific and southeast Asia regions.

In addition to outdoor air pollution, indoor smoke is a serious health risk for some 3 billion people who cook and heat their homes with biomass fuels and coal.

Water quality and health

Preventing the spread of water quality-related disease is a major global health challenge. According to the WHO, some of the major challenges include the following:

- Almost 1 billion people lack access to a safe, clean water supply.
- Two million annual deaths are attributable to unsafe water, sanitation and hygiene, and almost half of these are from diarrhoeal diseases.
- More than 50 countries still report cholera to the WHO.
- Schistosomiasis, a disease associated with parasitic worms that live in irrigation ditches and other water courses, has infected an estimated 260 million people.

Knowledge check 18

Explain how the implementation of good water practices could reduce the global disease burden.

A biologically transmitted disease: malaria

Prevalence and distribution

An estimated 3.2 billion people (40% of the world's population), in 100 countries, are at high risk of being infected with malaria and developing the disease. In 2014, an estimated 200 million cases of malaria occurred globally and the disease led to over 590,000 deaths. The burden is heaviest in the WHO African Region, where an estimated 90% of all malaria deaths occur. Children aged below 5 years account for almost 80% of all deaths.

Links to the physical environment

Malaria is caused by parasites of the species Plasmodium, which are spread from person to person through the bite of an infected mosquito — the transmission vector. These parasites are spread from one person to another by female mosquitoes of the genus Anopheles. Malaria transmission differs in intensity and regularity depending on local factors such as rainfall patterns, proximity of mosquito breeding sites and mosquito species. Some regions have a fairly constant number of cases throughout the year — these are malaria endemic — whereas in other areas there are 'malaria seasons', usually coinciding with the rainy season.

Malaria occurs in mainly tropical and subtropical regions where the disease is endemic in rainforest and savanna grasslands with at least 1,000 mm of rain per year, and often where the rainfall is seasonal. The parasite needs temperatures of 16–32°C to develop. The incidence of malaria decreases at altitudes over 1,500 m, hence some tropical areas are unaffected, such as the Kenyan Highlands. Like all mosquitoes, the Anopheles mosquito breeds well in warm or hot areas of stagnant, standing water, though drainage of these areas has reduced the disease's incidence. For similar reasons malaria is more common in coastal areas than inland.

Links to the socio-economic environment

Malaria exacts a heavy burden on the poorest and most vulnerable communities. It primarily affects low- and lower-/middle-income countries. Within countries where it is endemic, the poorest and most marginalised communities are the most severely affected, having the highest risks associated with malaria and the least access to effective services for prevention, diagnosis and treatment. A number of socio-economic variables are thought to have influenced a high incidence of malaria.

- **Housing quality:** densely clustered and overcrowded dwellings are linked to high incidences of the disease.
- **Unsanitary conditions in the community:** areas with standing dirty water, open waste flows and outlets encourage more mosquitoes.
- **Occupation:** some jobs are more prone to infection, such as farm workers and irrigation workers.
- **Levels of education:** researchers have found that, in general, people who have not completed their primary education are more likely to catch malaria.

Impact on health and wellbeing

The common symptoms — fever, headache, chills and vomiting — appear 10 to 15 days after a person is infected. If not treated promptly with effective medicines, malaria can cause severe illness that is often fatal.

There are further high personal impacts, such as the spending on insecticide-treated mosquito nets (ITNs), doctors' fees, drugs and transport to health facilities. Socially, malaria disrupts schooling and employment through absenteeism, and creates nutrition deficiencies and anaemia in children and women in malarial regions. As a result, 25% of first babies in some areas have a low birth weight.

In some countries with a very heavy malaria burden, the disease may account for as much as 40% of public health expenditure, 30–50% of inpatient admissions and up to 60% of outpatient visits.

Management and mitigation strategies

Malaria control and ultimately its elimination are inextricably linked with the strengthening of health systems, infrastructure development and poverty reduction. The main interventions include:

- vector controls (which reduce transmission by the mosquito from humans to mosquitoes and then back to humans), achieved using ITNs or indoor residual spraying (IRS)
- chemo-prevention (which prevents blood infections in humans)
- case management (which includes diagnosis and treatment of infections)

There has been an expansion in the use of diagnostic testing and the deployment of ACTs. This indicates a move away from treating people who have the disease to those who might have it. In 2015 a record number of long-lasting insecticidal nets (LLIN) were delivered to endemic countries in Africa. Another method is that pregnant women receive chemo-preventative treatment during their pregnancy in order to reduce child deaths.

Exam tip

In many examination questions key words such as physical, social and economic are used. Be clear as to their meaning.

Insecticide treated mosquito net (ITN) Protective nets that are treated with an insecticide, forming a protective barrier around people sleeping under them.

Indoor residual spraying (IRS) The application of insecticides to a person's dwelling, and on walls and other surfaces that serve as mosquito resting places.

ACT Artemisinin-based combination therapies for the treatment of malaria, combining two active ingredients with different methods of action. They are the most effective antimalarial treatment available today.

However, emerging drug and insecticide resistance continues to pose a major threat, and if left unaddressed, could trigger an upsurge in the disease. Resistance to artemisinin has been detected in southeast Asian countries, including Cambodia, Thailand and Vietnam.

In 2015, US scientists stated that they had bred a genetically modified mosquito that could resist malaria infection. If the laboratory technique works in the field, it could offer a new way of stopping the mosquitoes from spreading malaria.

> **Exam tip**
>
> If you have studied another biologically transmitted disease, make sure your notes follow the same sequence of headings.

A non-communicable disease: type 2 diabetes

Type 2 diabetes is one of a number of non-communicable diseases (NCDs). There are two types of diabetes:

- Type 1 diabetes occurs when the pancreas does not produce insulin. It can occur at any age, but usually before the age of 40. It is usually treated with insulin injections.
- Type 2 diabetes (T2D) occurs when the body doesn't produce enough insulin to function properly, or the body's cells don't react to insulin. It is much more common than Type 1 and is often linked with being overweight or obese.

Prevalence and distribution

According to the WHO:

- The total number of people in the world with T2D is projected to rise from 382 million in 2013 to 592 million in 2035.
- It is estimated that 80% of the people who have T2D live in developing countries.
- T2D accounted for 11% of global health expenditure in 2013 (US$548 billion), a figure expected to be over US$600 billion in 2035.
- T2D is associated with roughly 8% of total world mortality, about the same as HIV/AIDS and malaria combined.
- Mortality and disability associated with T2D are particularly high in poor- and middle-income countries where people are unlikely to get the treatment that helps prevent the worst complications of the disease.

Links to the physical environment

Links between most, if not all, NCDs to the physical environment are difficult to establish. Scientists have tried to examine if there is a link with air quality in urban areas, and with varying temperature levels around the world. No such links have been established. Increased temperatures within an urban area, leading to heat stress, could add to the pressures already placed on a body due to being overweight or obese. Similarly, difficulty of breathing in a polluted environment could add further stress. However, these are both exacerbating factors rather than direct causes.

Links to the socio-economic environment

The WHO states that too much weight gain and obesity are 'driving' the global T2D epidemic. Recent estimates suggest that 1 billion people in the developing world are obese. There are a number of factors contributing to this.

- **Diet:** high calorie intake is the main factor leading to obesity. In developing countries rapid economic development has introduced a more 'Western' diet, with less fruit and fewer vegetables, combined with a higher intake of carbohydrates, fatty foods, salt and sugar.
- **Urban lifestyles:** rates of urbanisation in the developing world are considerably higher than elsewhere. Urbanisation tends to mean a more sedentary lifestyle, with a low level of physical activity.
- **Tobacco use:** smoking is a key risk factor linked to T2D. An estimated 50–60% of adult males in developing countries are regular smokers.
- **Stress:** stress increases blood sugar levels, raises blood pressure and can suppress the digestive process. Raised blood sugar levels are a key risk factor in the development of T2D.

> **Exam tip**
>
> In many examination questions key words such as physical, social and economic are used. Be clear as to their meaning.

Impact on health and wellbeing

Diabetes cannot be cured but can be managed with a mixture of medication and lifestyle change. Longer term it can lead to heart disease, kidney failure, blindness and, in extreme cases, amputation of limbs. As most healthcare costs in developing countries must be paid by patients out of their own pockets, the cost of healthcare for T2D creates a significant strain on household budgets, particularly for low-income families.

Management and mitigation strategies

Public awareness of T2D is slowly increasing in many developing countries. In Sri Lanka, for example, awareness is increasing mainly because of local media coverage and the activities of the Diabetes Association of Sri Lanka (DASL). DASL has a walk-in centre in the capital, Colombo, where individuals can be screened or take part in structured health programmes at a modest cost. The centre also provides information through workshops, a website and printed materials. DASL is also spreading the message that exercise can help reduce the threat of T2D. Exercise areas are being created in many urban centres within the country.

> **Exam tip**
>
> If you have studied another NCD, make sure your notes follow the same sequence of headings.

The role of international agencies and NGOs
The World Health Organization (WHO)

The WHO is an agency of the United Nations (UN), established in 1948 and based in Geneva. The work of the WHO includes:

- providing a central clearing house for information and research on such features as vaccines, cancer research, nutrition, drug addiction and nuclear radiation hazards
- sponsoring measures for the control of epidemics and endemic diseases by promoting mass campaigns involving vaccination programmes, instruction on the use of antibiotics and insecticides, assistance in providing pure water supplies and sanitation systems, and health education for rural populations
- advising on the prevention and treatment of both infectious diseases and NCDs
- working with other UN agencies (such as UNAIDS and UNICEF) and NGOs on international health issues and crises (such as the Ebola crisis in 2014/15)

Non-governmental organisations (NGOs)

A number of NGOs operate in the field of world health. In some developing countries they often act as alternative healthcare providers to the state, and during times of crisis they will provide the initial set of responses, certainly in remote areas. They are largely funded by donations from the developed world, mostly by individuals or organisations rather than by nations. One such NGO is Médecins Sans Frontières (MSF).

Knowledge check 19

Describe the work of one identified NGO.

Population change

Factors in natural population change

Fertility

In most parts of the world fertility exceeds both mortality and migration and is therefore the main determinant of population growth. Several African countries have very high crude birth rates of over 40 per 1,000 per year. These include Burkina Faso, Burundi, Mali and Niger. At the other end of the scale China, Japan, Singapore and Spain have birth rates of less than 12 per 1,000 per year. Fertility varies for a number of reasons:

- Some countries in sub-Saharan Africa have high birth rates to counter the high rates of infant mortality (often over 70 per 1,000 live births per year).
- In many parts of the world, tradition and culture demand high rates of reproduction. Here the opinion of women has little influence weighed against intense cultural expectations. One indicator of this is child marriage. Over 60% of women in some countries of sub-Saharan Africa and parts of Asia are married before the age of 18.
- A key determinant is education, especially female literacy. Knowledge of birth control and more opportunity for employment lower birth rates.
- Economic factors are important, especially in developing countries where children are seen as an economic asset. They are viewed as producers rather than consumers. In developed countries this general perception is reversed and the high cost of the child dependency years is often a reason for deferring child rearing.
- Religion is of major significance, as both the Muslim and Roman Catholic religions oppose artificial birth control.
- There have been instances where politics have influenced fertility. These have been either to increase the population (as in Russia and Romania) or to decrease it (as in China with its one-child policy, although this has now been abandoned).

Mortality

Some of the highest crude death rates are found in developing countries, particularly in sub-Saharan Africa. The Central African Republic, Democratic Republic of Congo, Lesotho and Mali all have death rates of 15 per 1,000 or more. On the other hand, some of the lowest mortality rates are found in countries with a wide range of economic development, for example Andorra, Brunei, Costa Rica and the Maldives. Mortality varies for a number of reasons:

Natural population change Population change arising from the relationship between crude birth rates and crude death rates. It is usually indicated as a percentage.

Fertility rate The number of live births per 1,000 women aged 15–49 per year.

Crude birth rate The number of live births per 1,000 population per year.

Crude death rate The number of deaths per 1,000 population per year.

- Areas with high rates of **infant mortality** have high rates of mortality. Infant mortality is a prime indicator of socio-economic development and in some areas it is very high, for example Sierra Leone has a rate of 92 per 1,000 live births.
- Areas of higher levels of medical infrastructure have lower levels of mortality.
- Poverty, poor nutrition and a lack of clean water and sanitation (all associated with low levels of economic development) all increase mortality rates.

Around the world, mortality has fallen steadily due to medical advances. It has been suggested that the world is more willing to control mortality than it is to control fertility.

The Demographic Transition Model (DTM)

The Demographic Transition Model (DTM) is based on the notion that population change over time is closely linked to economic development. It can be used to predict how nations follow a demographic pathway as their economic development progresses.

The model shows how a country's population total will change over time as a result of variations in the birth and death rate. Therefore, it focuses entirely on natural change — migration is not a feature of the DTM. The greater the difference between the birth rate and the death rate, the faster the rate of natural increase and thus the steeper the curve in the growth of total population. The model suggests that, over time, populations will show a transition from low numbers, high fertility and high mortality to a high total population with low fertility and low mortality. A Stage 5 was added in the 1990s and is an accepted part of the model today.

The five stages of the model are as follows:
- **Stage 1 (High fluctuating):** a period of high birth rates and high death rates, both of which fluctuate. Population growth is small.
- **Stage 2 (Early expanding):** a period of high birth rates but falling death rates. The population begins to expand rapidly.
- **Stage 3 (Late expanding):** a period of falling birth rates and continuing falling death rates. Population continues to grow but at a slower rate.
- **Stage 4 (Low fluctuating):** a period of low birth rates and low death rates, both of which fluctuate. Population growth is small.
- **Stage 5 (Decline):** a later period when death rates slightly exceed birth rates, which causes a population to decline.

Application of the model in contrasting settings

The model directly connects demographic change with social and economic change — there is no attempt to put it into a physical setting. In Stage 1 a poor, agriculturally based, subsistence society is limited in its ability to prevent mortality when food is short or outbreaks of disease occur. A high birth rate will therefore be counteracted by a high death rate.

Stage 2 marks a period of increasing national wealth and as a result there is a significant decline in death rates. In the UK, from 1600, there was an agricultural revolution, and by 1750 food supply exceeded population demand. The Industrial Revolution then followed. This brought about dreadful working conditions in factories and poverty in rapidly urbanising cities, such as Manchester, but alongside these there were also massive improvements in public health and medical care. So, overall,

Infant mortality rate
The number of children under the age of 1 year who die per 1,000 live births per year.

Exam tip
The World Population Data Sheet produced by the Population Reference Bureau (www.prb.org/) enables you to keep up to date with all of these key vital rates.

Exam tip
Most textbooks have a diagram of the DTM. Study it closely.

mortality continued to fall. Today, countries with limited economic development have been able to move into Stage 2 due to the transfer of technology and provision of benefits, such as vaccination programmes, better maternal and neonatal care and more efficient farming practices. Thus, a reduction in mortality does not necessarily correlate with economic growth in the country itself. External help may provide the stimulus for change.

The model suggests that further increases in wealth cause a fall in birth rate and progression to Stages 3 and 4. Once children are no longer seen as an economic necessity fewer will be born. However, the model underplays the importance of political and cultural factors that affect fertility. Birth rates have been slow to fall in countries where there is religious pressure to have children, for example some Islamic and Catholic countries.

As stated earlier, the model makes no specific reference to the impact of migration on population change. The fall in death rates attributed to economic growth in western Europe was also helped by emigration — large numbers of people left Italy and Ireland, for example, for the New World in the mid-nineteenth and early twentieth centuries, and this relieved some pressure on land resources. The progress of some developing countries through the demographic transition is currently slow or even static. Developing countries such as Botswana, Lesotho and Swaziland, which have a high incidence of HIV/AIDS, have maintained high death rates despite signs of economic progress.

The demographic dividend

The concept of the demographic dividend was introduced earlier in this book (page 29). A country's fertility rate falls during its demographic transition as a country's level of development increases. The result is fewer dependent children and relatively more productive young adults in the population. A large body of young and healthy people with high aspirations can boost economic growth, provided there is investment in education and employment, and little emigration. The demographic dividend played an important role in the emergence of the **Asian Tiger** economies during the 1960s and is one reason for China's rapid economic growth in recent decades.

In such cases, the transition of large, youthful cohorts into working age, accompanied by falling birth rates, boosts economic and social development because of the following:

- A large, young workforce serves as a powerful magnet for 'footloose' global companies to invest in the country.
- Workers with fewer children begin investing some of their income, contributing to financial growth.
- Women become more likely to enter the formal workforce, promoting greater gender equality.
- Salaried workers quickly become consumers, so global retailers and media corporations view these countries as important emerging markets.

However, a demographic dividend is not always delivered when population structure changes. Due to a lack of social development, some countries fail to make the most of their human resources. A large working-age population is a wasted opportunity if levels of education, especially numeracy and literacy, are weak. Good governance is essential.

Knowledge check 20

How might a country regress through the Demographic Transition Model (DTM)?

Asian Tigers The countries of Hong Kong, Singapore, South Korea and Taiwan.

Knowledge check 21

Explain how changing lifestyles may affect the demographic dividend.

Age-sex composition

Population structure refers to the make-up of the population of a country. The most studied form of structure is that of age and sex composition and is represented by a population pyramid.

Standard population pyramids can be drawn to represent each stage of the DTM and the structures of individual countries are often compared with these pyramids. In simple terms, the stages are as follows.

- **Stage 1:** has a triangular shape, which shows a wide base (indicating a high birth rate) and sloping sides (indicating a high death rate) forming a peak with few elderly.
- **Stage 2:** the sides become slightly more steep, showing a decrease in the death rate.
- **Stage 3:** the sides are steep but the base is less wide. showing a decline in the birth rate.
- **Stage 4:** a dome-shape — the sides are steep all the way up to the 65 age group and there is an increase in the height of the pyramid, showing more older people.
- **Stage 5:** the base narrows further, showing the recent lower birth rate.

Population structure is closely linked to dependency. From this, some writers prefer to discuss either:

- a **youthful population**, which has a large number of younger people in proportion to the working population. This puts pressure on education, housing and maternal health services.
- an **ageing population**, where there are a large number of older people in proportion to the working population. This puts pressure on the working population to work longer and the age of attaining a pension may have to rise to provide the increasing numbers of older people with pensions and old-age care.

Cultural controls

A number of cultural controls on population change have been referred to in the previous sections.

- **Attitudes to women:** women are discriminated against in many cultures, either openly or implicitly. Features such as low levels of education, early marriage (even child marriage) and forced/arranged marriages are common.
- **Gender preferences:** also feature in many societies, for example the desire for a male heir. This preference can be loosely based on economic factors, for example the need for a male to till the land. However, it can be based on societal norms — families may continue to procreate until they have a son, and in some extreme cases, female infanticide has taken place.
- **Religion:** a key influence in demographic trends. This influences attitudes to artificial contraception and abortion. In some African, Arabian and North American societies polygamy is prevalent.

> **Exam tip**
> Most textbooks have diagrams of population pyramids associated with each stage of the DTM. Study them closely.

Dependency ratio The relationship between the economically active (working) population and the non-economically active (dependent) population.

International migration

When examining population change, the balance between immigration and emigration (net migration) must also be considered. Migration can be local or within a country, in which case it will not change the overall population total for any country. International migration does, however, change the total population of a country. It is estimated that there are over 200 million international migrants in the world.

Economic migrants form by far the greatest proportion of international migrants. It is thought that poverty drives the typical 'economic migrant'. There are numerous examples of movements of economic migrants over recent times:

- In the late nineteenth and early twentieth century transatlantic migrations involved the movement of large numbers of people from Europe to North America. Migrants moved from countries such as Ireland, Italy or Norway where they were experiencing immense poverty, to the new industrialising economy of the USA, where 'fortunes could be made'.
- Since 1980 there have been substantial increases in migration to western Europe, firstly from countries such as Greece, Portugal and Spain, then from North and West Africa, and most recently from central and eastern Europe.
- During 2015 and 2016 thousands of migrants fled Afghanistan, Iraq, Libya and Syria to seek refuge in European countries. When questioned about where they wanted to go, many said Germany, the richest country within the EU.

Much smaller proportions of people are forced to move as asylum seekers and refugees, although the numbers are still large. The United Nations High Commissioner for Refugees (UNHCR) estimated that there were over 18 million refugees in 2015. Refugees are unable (or unwilling) to return to their country of origin for fear of persecution. Historically, countries affected by civil war, by persecution of minority groups on grounds of religion or ethnicity, or governed by political regimes that punish dissent have all produced large refugee populations.

In simple terms, a refugee is a successful asylum seeker. There has been a worldwide growth in applications for asylum. The UNHCR reported that 1.3 million people submitted asylum applications in 2014. It is then up to the government of the receiving country to decide if they qualify as refugees and should be allowed to stay. In 2014, the highest number of asylum applications was submitted in Germany, followed by the USA and South Africa. The UK was eighth in the world with over 24,000 applications, mostly people from Iran, Pakistan, Sri Lanka and Syria.

Causes of international migration

Various factors are said to influence international migration.

- **Push factors:** these are the negative aspects of the current place of residence. They include factors such as lack of employment, low wages, poor housing, poor educational opportunities, political persecution, natural hazards, starvation and war.
- **Pull factors:** these are the attractions of the place of destination. Often they are the inverse of the push factors: better employment and educational opportunities, better housing and social services, higher wages, family integration and political stability.

Net migration The difference between the numbers of in-migrants and out-migrants.

Migration Involves a permanent or semi-permanent change of residence.

International migration The movement of people across national frontiers, for a minimum of 1 year.

Economic migrant A person who moves voluntarily for work or to improve his/her social conditions.

Asylum seeker A person who has applied for refugee status and is waiting for a decision as to whether or not they qualify.

Refugee A person who, owing to a fear of being persecuted for reasons of race, religion, nationality, membership of a particular social group or political opinion, has fled his/her country and sought protection in another country.

Knowledge check 22

Where are the major sources of refugees in the world today?

■ **Perception:** this is the subjective view, or image, that a person has of an environment, derived from personal experience, the experience of others and from the media. If the perceived push or pull factors are strong enough to overcome the forces of inertia (cost of moving, disruption of social networks), migration will occur. It is often this image, rather than objective reality, that is the basis of the decision-making process.

It is no surprise that migration should be growing in an increasingly interconnected world. The combination of technological change, improved transport infrastructure and economic growth has made mobility easier and more desirable to many.

Implications of international migration

International migration continues to be a contentious area of public debate. It is seen at best as a problem to be addressed, and at worst as the source of a wider set of social and economic issues. As a result, both the general public and policymakers continue to ask why people move, and what can be done to discourage this movement. It has caused significant demographic, environmental, social, economic, health and political implications (see Table 9).

Table 9 Demographic, environmental, social, economic, health and political implications of international migration

Factor	Implication for country of origin	Implication for country of destination
Demographic	■ Reduction in birth rate ■ Imbalanced population structure — ageing population	■ Increase in birth rate ■ Imbalanced population structure/youthful population
Environmental	■ Abandonment of land and houses	■ Pressure on land for new housing stock
Social	■ Reduced pressure on social services (health/education) ■ Loss of skills ('brain drain')	■ Increased pressure on social services (health/education) ■ Multiculturalism benefits/ issues
Economic	■ Reduced levels of unemployment ■ Remittances sent home ■ New skills introduced by returnees	■ Skills shortages and employment vacancies filled ■ Cheap source of labour ■ Tax benefits to the state ■ Demographic dividend created (see page 44)
Health	■ Reduced pressure on health facilities	■ Increase in incidence and variety of infectious diseases ■ Increased pressure on health services ■ The issue of 'health tourism'
Political	■ Issues regarding declining regions — investment needed?	■ Arguments to reduce immigration ■ Rise of right-wing political parties

Exam tip

When analysing or evaluating any of these implications, try to support the points you make with reference to specific issues and/or locations.

Principles of population ecology and their application to human populations

Population growth dynamics

The key parameters of population growth dynamics are birth and death rates. As we have seen, the number of births in a population is limited not only by biological factors (for example ages of both the male and especially the female of the species), but also by cultural factors, such as age of marriage and attitudes to contraception. Also, it was noted that one important factor influencing birth rates was a specific death rate: infant mortality. If offspring are more likely to die young, then birth rates increase to compensate. Such parameters are also seen in the natural world, and hence some writers have linked population growth to ecology, i.e. the natural world. Furthermore, as in the natural world, human populations are affected by uncontrollable events which may impact on them — for example, natural hazards and disease. Changes in food supply have also impacted human populations in the past, and still do have an effect in some developing areas of the world, such as the famines in East Africa in the last century. Some scientists have translated this into ecological statements:

- When biotic potential (the reproductive capacity) is greater than environmental resistance (limiting factors such as famine and disease), then there is population growth.
- Similarly, if limiting factors outweigh biotic potential, then populations will decline.

Overpopulation, underpopulation and optimum population

It is estimated that the world's population will reach 9 billion before 2050. For many years, during which the world's population has continued to grow, people have questioned whether the world has enough resources to cope with ever-increasing numbers of people. When studying the balance between population and resources, three concepts can be considered:

- **Overpopulation** occurs where the population is too large for the resources available. This relationship also depends on the level of technology available to help to make good use of resources, as well as on the climate and physical limitations of the area. Overpopulation can cause unemployment and out-migration.
- **Underpopulation** occurs where there are not enough people living in an area or country to utilise the resources efficiently. An increase in the number of people would therefore result in a higher standard of living. Underpopulated areas tend to have in-migration and low unemployment.
- **Optimum population** is stated to exist where the resources available can be developed efficiently in order to satisfy the needs of the current population and provide the highest standard of living. However, as technology develops, the optimum population will increase. This theoretical concept has not been achieved anywhere in the world.

Exam tip

One way of illustrating these population concepts is to draw a simple line graph with GDP per capita on the y-axis, and total population on the x-axis. Try to draw it.

Implications of population size and structure for the balance between population and resources

These can be examined in the context of a country, for example Japan (population 127 million).

Population decline has started to take place in Japan and will continue into the future. The cause is purely natural — death rates (10 per 1,000) exceed birth rates (8 per 1,000). Experts attribute Japan's population decline to the high cost of raising children in the country, the growing number of women who choose to work longer and have a career rather than have children, and Japan's reluctance to accept immigrants.

Whether or not such population decline is a problem that needs a solution is open to debate. Population decline has many benefits, but in Japan it will also present significant problems. It is already affecting rural areas in particular. In addition to low birth rates, rural areas tend to experience significant outflows of young people who move to urban areas. Rural depopulation in Japan is driven by young people being drawn to the life, education and employment opportunities of urban areas. A consequence of this depopulation is the increasing amount of abandoned houses, and their associated land, left unoccupied when the last resident dies.

The increasingly inverted structure of Japan's population pyramid, with fewer young people than old people, means that it will be very difficult to generate the tax revenues necessary to pay for the healthcare needs of the elderly. Japan's older population (over 65) is currently around 25% of the total. In 2050, this proportion is expected to be 40%. In rural areas, it is not uncommon to find towns in which 35% or more of the population is over 65. As the elderly population grows, the financial burden of healthcare in Japan will become substantial, and there could very well be a shortage of labour in the healthcare industry.

It is possible that Japan's population will drop to just 96 million by 2050. While birth incentives and immigration incentives are often suggested as the solution to bring the young workers necessary to support the country's ageing population, there is a national reluctance for either of these to take place. Slowing population growth and an ageing population are shrinking its pool of taxable citizens, causing the social welfare costs to spiral upwards. This has led to Japan becoming the most indebted industrial nation in the world.

The concepts of carrying capacity and ecological footprint

The **carrying capacity** of an area refers to the largest population that the resources of a given environment can support. Development, the living standards of people and in turn the consumption patterns of a population also influence carrying capacity. The latter is also a function of attitudes. As a society becomes more 'Westernised',

> **Exam tip**
>
> You could analyse another country in order to examine the links between population size/structure and resources. Good examples would be a Gulf state (high immigration) or a sub-Saharan country (young population).

consumption rates increase. This can be evidenced by the increasing consumer consumption rates of people in emerging economies, such as China and India, for designer goods.

An **ecological footprint** refers to a measurement of the area of land and/or water required to provide a person (or society) with the energy, food and other resources they consume, and render the waste they produce harmless. Using this assessment, it is possible to estimate how much of the Earth (or how many planet Earths) it would take to support humanity if everybody lived a given lifestyle (and consumption rate). You can calculate your own personal ecological footprint using the website http://ecologicalfootprint.com/.

Some have developed these ideas by suggesting that each year should have an 'Earth Overshoot Day' — the day when the productive capacity of the planet has been used up for that calendar year. In 2000 it was 1 November, while in 2016 it was 8 August.

The Population, Resources and Pollution model

Human activities can affect both the biotic (natural) and abiotic (physical) conditions of an environment. As human culture has developed over time from hunting and gathering to agriculture and then into industrial societies, the impact on these environmental conditions has grown to a level that many believe is unsustainable. The **Population, Resources and Pollution (PRP)** model illustrates several important relationships between people and their environment, and offers a 'big picture' view of human–environment interactions.

The PRP model shows that humans, like all other organisms, acquire resources from the environment. The acquisition of resources, for example through coal mining, alters both the biotic and abiotic environment. Surface coal mines cause deforestation and disrupt habitats. They can also lead to soil erosion that pollutes nearby steams. Hence there is a link in the model between resource acquisition and pollution (see Figure 5).

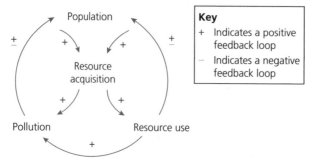

Figure 5 The Population, Resources and Pollution model

Resources extracted from the ground are then put to use. For example, after being mined, coal is burned in power stations. Other minerals extracted from the ground are also fashioned into finished products, such as motor vehicles and machinery. Such activities can produce pollution, indicated in the model by the link between resource use and pollution.

The model also contains examples of negative and positive feedback loops. Some of the negative feedback loops shown on the PRP model are of concern to environmentalists. For example, continued soil erosion from the world's farmlands resulting from poor agricultural practices such as overgrazing (and due to population pressures in the first place) could cause a marked decline in food production, which could have an effect on the global population.

On the other hand, positive feedback is shown when resource acquisition and use, especially that permitted by technology, can promote population growth. The efficient harvest of food has made it possible for larger numbers of people to inhabit the Earth.

Contrasting perspectives on population growth

Various theories have been put forward to explain the relationship between population and resources. The theories are sometimes categorised as being either pessimistic or optimistic.

The case for pessimism: Thomas Malthus

Thomas Malthus stated in his 1798 work 'An Essay on the Principle of Population' that population growth was geometric (1, 2, 4, 8, 16 etc.) while food supply could only grow arithmetically (1, 2, 3, 4, 5). This, inevitably, leads to a point where carrying capacity is exceeded, leading to a food shortage. Malthus believed that increasing the food supply dramatically was not possible, and so food shortages would lead to a series of population checks, which would reduce the population size. These checks would either increase the death rate (a 'positive check') or reduce the birth rate (a 'preventative check'). Examples of positive checks include war, famine and epidemic. Preventative checks occur when individuals realise that there may not be enough food to support a family, and so they opt for later marriages or sexual abstinence (note, this was before the days of artificial contraception). Malthus believed a series of cycles would occur, in which carrying capacity was exceeded, each leading to a period of population check. Malthus argued pessimistically that preventative checks would never reduce the population sufficiently and that we would never escape from cruel positive checks. In other words, starvation, war and disease are inevitable.

In 1972, 'The Limits to Growth' report, produced by the **neo-Malthusian Club of Rome**, suggested that there would be a sudden decline in global population in 100 years due to the overuse of resources. The decrease in population would return the world to a state of balance with the resources on the land.

The case for optimism: Ester Boserup

Ester Boserup, a UN agricultural economist, argued in 1965 that it was the size of a population that determined the level of its food supply. By examining the development

Negative feedback loops Act in such a way to nullify any change that has taken place. They are the main means of controlling biological systems and regulating equilibrium.

Positive feedback loops Act in such a way that one change leads to a further change, which in turn stimulates the first one in a repetitive cycle. In this way change is perpetuated.

Knowledge check 23

Give an example of when positive feedback in the Population, Resources and Pollution (PRP) model can create environmental problems.

of agriculture in a number of regions, Boserup concluded that as population size reached carrying capacity, societies were forced to make radical agricultural changes to ensure there was enough food. For example, Boserup noted that the people of Java in Indonesia had over time adapted their farming practices several times to feed a larger population. They had moved from long fallow farming (land is farmed for 1–3 years and then left to recover for 10–20 years) to short fallow, and then to annual cropping (a crop is harvested annually from a piece of land) to multiple cropping (a piece of land produces more than one annual crop). Such optimists do not regard population size as a problem, because humans can invent solutions to any food shortages. They argue that agricultural advances over the last century, such as the Green Revolution and more recently the development of genetically modified foods, show this. In essence, 'necessity is the mother of invention'.

Other writers have continued this optimistic theme. **Julian Simon** summed up the optimistic perspective in his book *The Ultimate Resource* (1981) by suggesting that the ultimate resource is human ingenuity.

> **Exam tip**
> You could research the views of other writers on this controversial topic such as Stephen Emmott, Bjorn Lomborg and Danny Dorling.

Global population futures

Health impacts of global environmental change

A number of impacts on human health have been identified as the Earth's environment undergoes change and as populations grow. They can be categorised under the headings of ozone depletion and climate change.

Ozone depletion

The ozone layer shields the Earth from most of the harmful ultraviolet radiation from the sun. It is this radiation that causes an increase in the incidence of skin cancer and eye cataracts. **Ozone depletion** occurs when the rate at which the ozone layer is formed is less than the rate at which it is destroyed. In recent years, this depletion has manifested itself by the emergence of a 'hole' in the ozone layer over Antarctica and the Arctic. The damage is believed to have been caused by the use of chlorofluorocarbons (CFCs) in refrigeration and insulation, which break down ozone, although EU and other countries have now banned their use.

Skin cancer is a disease associated with exposure to the sun, and made worse by more UV radiation reaching the surface through ozone 'holes'. Rates of malignant melanoma vary around the world, with Australia being the worst affected. In the UK, the incidence of skin cancer has increased within the over-55 age group, or the 'sun, sand and sangria generation', as its rise has been linked to the cheap package holiday boom to southern Europe that dates from the 1960s.

Cataracts are a form of eye damage that can eventually lead to blindness if not treated. As with skin cancer, increasing rates of cataracts have been linked to UV radiation. Incidence rates are greater in tropical areas, at higher altitudes where UV levels are higher, and also where the UV radiation can be reflected into the eye from light surfaces such as snow.

> **Ozone layer** A concentration of the gas ozone located in the stratosphere at an altitude of between 10 km and 50 km above sea level.

Climate change

The WHO has estimated that up to a quarter of a million more people will die per year as a result of climate change. Such a figure will be impossible to verify. Climate change is likely to have impacts on health in several ways:

- Direct impacts from extreme weather events such as more frequent and severe storms and floods, and heat waves.
- Indirect impacts from environmental and ecological change such as:
  - **Thermal stress:** hot and humid summer weather can cause illness, such as dehydration, heat exhaustion and heat stroke, and death. Heat waves also exacerbate other health risks such as smog, fires and vermin infestations. Older adults, people with chronic medical conditions and the socially isolated are most vulnerable.
  - **Emergent and changing distributions of vector-borne diseases:** it is predicted that the prevalence of diseases such as malaria and dengue fever will increase as the mosquito vectors spread further around the world following warmer and wetter weather. Areas most at risk include China, Mexico, Turkey and the southern USA. Further, it is thought that other emergent diseases could have a greater incidence such as the Zika virus in Latin America, the West Nile virus in North America and Lyme disease in Europe (including the UK).
  - **Agricultural productivity:** some areas, such as higher latitudes, will see an increase in crop yields, in the variety of crops (such as maize and soya beans) that can be grown and in the length of the growing season. On the other hand, in some lower latitudes there will be greater incidence of thermal stress for plants and livestock, and yields may fall.
  - **Nutritional standards:** in the developed world it is suggested that there will be a decline in red meat consumption, which will also benefit the environment through less livestock production and less forest clearance. However, crop failure in areas most at risk from the damaging effects of climate change will have a negative impact on the nutrition of the people living there.

> **Exam tip**
>
> When analysing or evaluating any of these impacts, try to support the points you make with references to specific issues and/or locations.

Prospects for global population

The world's population will continue to grow more slowly than in the recent past. In 2000, world population grew by 1.24% per year. In 2015, it grew by 1.18% per year — still an additional 83 million people annually. It is projected to increase by more than 1 billion people within the next 15 years, reaching 8.5 billion in 2030, and to increase further to 9.7 billion in 2050 and 11.2 billion by 2100 (see Table 10).

Table 10 Present and projected population totals by region (2015–2100)

Area of world	2015 (millions)	2050 (millions)	2100 (millions)
Africa	1,186	2,478	4,387
Asia	4,393	5,267	4,889
Europe	738	707	646
Latin America and Caribbean	634	784	721
North America	358	433	500
Oceania	39	57	71
World	7,349	9,725	11,213

Source: UN Population Division (2015)

Projected distributions

More than half of global population growth between now and 2050 is expected to occur in Africa. Africa has the highest rate of population growth, growing at 2.6% per year. Consequently, of the additional 2.4 billion people projected to be added to the global population between 2015 and 2050, 1.3 billion will be in Africa.

Asia is projected to be the second-largest contributor to future global population growth, adding 0.9 billion people between 2015 and 2050, followed by North America, Latin America and the Caribbean, and Oceania. Europe is projected to have a smaller population in 2050 than in 2015 (see Table 10).

Knowledge check 24

How will the populations of China, India and Nigeria change in the future?

Critical appraisal of future population–environment relationships

The developed world

The populations of most European countries will decline in the next generation, and in the cases of Germany, Japan and Russia, the decline will be dramatic. The contraction of the population, particularly during the transitional period before the older generations die off, will leave a relatively small number of workers supporting a very large group of retirees, particularly as life expectancy in advanced industrial countries increases. In addition, it may be left to the smaller, younger generation to pay off the national debts the older generation incurred.

The most obvious solution to this problem is immigration. However, one major issue is that some Westernised countries have cultural problems integrating immigrants. This was evidenced in Europe during and after the recent EU referendum campaign in the UK, and although the Europeans have tried to integrate immigrants — particularly those from the Islamic world — they have overall found it a challenge. While Japan does not have a history of integrating migrants, the USA has historical sources of immigration, particularly from Mexico. However, some right-wing politicians within the USA now want to restrict migration from Mexico.

Life expectancy At birth, the average age to which a person is expected to live.

The developing world

When Western countries went through their demographic transition, both mortality and fertility fell gradually over a period of a century or more. Since the 1960s, demographers have been surprised to see how fast the equivalent transition happened in Asia and Latin America. In countries like China and Brazil, it took just three or four decades for the fertility rate to plunge from more than six to less than two. The experience in Asia and Latin America led demographers to expect a similarly rapid transition in Africa. However, this has not been the case. Over the past decade or two, it has become clear that fertility is falling much more slowly in some countries in sub-Saharan Africa, such as Nigeria, than it did on other continents. According to the UN, of the people added to the planet in this century, one in five will be Nigerian.

There is, however, another variable that needs to be considered when examining future population growth: education. Educating girls in particular has been found to be one of the best ways of bringing down fertility in the long term. However, progress

Exam tip

This is a very topical area of study. Try to keep up to date with it.

in female education is slow, and governments in Africa and elsewhere need to make access to family planning more widely available. Education is the key to global population and environmental futures.

Case studies

You are required to study **one country/society experiencing specific patterns of population change** to illustrate and analyse the character, scale and patterns of change that have taken place. You should include relevant environmental and socio-economic factors, and analyse the implications for that country/society. Examples could include the ageing population of Japan, or the migration of eastern Europeans into the UK.

You are also required to study **a specified local area** to illustrate and analyse the relationship between place and health to its environment, socio-economic character, and the experience and attitudes of its population. Examples could include the work of health charities in specific villages in the developing world, or a field study and/or online research based on local communities within the UK.

Summary

After studying this topic, you should be able to:

- understand the environmental contexts for population, both physical (e.g. climate, soils) and human (e.g. development, causes of change) and their impact on population numbers and densities
- know and understand the global patterns of food supply, the agricultural systems that produce it and the factors that cause variations in it, such as climate and soil types
- explain how climate change and soil problems can impact on food supply and food security
- know and understand the patterns of world health, and the economic, social and environmental factors that cause variations in it

- know and understand the causes, impacts and strategies to manage and mitigate two different diseases — one biologically transmitted and one non-communicable
- explain how population changes over time, and assess the impact of contrasting physical and human settings on population change
- analyse the reasons for, and consequences of, international migration
- understand the links between population dynamics and ecology, and evaluate the various theories associated with the link between population and resources
- examine the prospects for future population growth within a changing climate, with particular regard to health matters and population–environment relationships

Questions & Answers

Assessment overview

In this section of the book, two sets of questions on each of the content areas are given: for Hazards there is one set for AS and one for A-level, and for Population and the environment there are two sets of questions for A-level. For each of these, the style of questions used in the examination papers has been replicated, with a mixture of multiple-choice questions, short-answer, data-stimulus questions and extended prose questions. Other than the multiple-choice questions and some short knowledge-based questions, all questions will be assessed using a 'levels of response' mark scheme, to a maximum of four levels. The relative proportions and weightings of these questions varies between AS and A-level.

Each set of questions in this section is structured as follows:

- Sample questions in the style of the examination
- Mark schemes in the style of the examination
- Exemplar student answers at a high level
- Examiner's commentary on each of the above

For AS and A-level geography, all assessments will test one or more of the following Assessment Objectives (AOs):

- **AO1:** Demonstrate knowledge and understanding of places, environments, concepts, processes, interactions and change, at a variety of scales.
- **AO2:** Apply knowledge and understanding in different contexts to interpret, analyse and evaluate geographical information and issues.
- **AO3:** Use a variety of relevant quantitative, qualitative and fieldwork skills to investigate geographical questions and issues, interpret, analyse and evaluate data and evidence, construct arguments and draw conclusions.

All questions that carry a large number of marks (at AS and A-level) require candidates to consider connections between the subject matter and other aspects of geography, or develop deeper understanding, in order to access the highest marks. The former was referred to as synopticity, but is now known as **connections** — in other words, try to think of connections or **links** between the subject matter you are writing about and other areas of the specification. In some cases the required links will be indicated in the question.

For **AS** Hazards, 40 marks are available and the breakdown of questions is:

- Two 1-mark multiple-choice questions (AO1 or AO3)
- One 3-mark question (AO1)
- One 6-mark question with data — marked to two levels (AO3)
- One 9-mark question requiring extended prose responses marked to three levels (AO1/AO2)
- One 20-mark question requiring extended prose responses marked to four levels (AO1/AO2)

Note that the latter two questions may have an explicit connection to another part of the specification.

You should allocate **one minute** per mark to answer the written-answer questions.

For **A-level**, Hazards and Population and the environment are worth 48 marks each, and the breakdown of questions per topic is:

- Four 1-mark multiple-choice questions (AO1 or AO3)
- One 6-mark question with data — marked to two levels (AO3)
- One 9-mark question requiring extended prose responses marked to three levels (AO1/AO2)
- One 9-mark question requiring extended prose responses marked to three levels (AO1/AO2)
- One 20-mark question requiring extended prose responses marked to four levels (AO1/AO2)

Note that the latter two questions may have an explicit connection to another part of the specification.

You should allocate **one and a half minutes** per mark to answer the written questions.

For each sample question, one answer has been provided at the upper end of the mark range. Study carefully the descriptions of the 'levels' given in the mark schemes and understand the requirements (or 'triggers') necessary to move an answer from one level to the next. You should also read the commentary with the mark schemes to understand why credit has or has not been awarded. In all cases, actual marks are indicated.

The extended response writing tasks at both AS and A-level, which each carry 20 marks, will be assessed using a generic mark scheme such as the one below. Study this carefully to see what is needed to move from one level to the next.

Note: AS questions are not available for Population and the environment.

Level/Mark range	Criteria/Descriptor
Level 4 (16–20 marks)	■ Detailed evaluative conclusion that is rational and firmly based on knowledge and understanding, which is applied to the context of the question (AO2). ■ Detailed, coherent and relevant analysis and evaluation in the application of knowledge and understanding throughout (AO2). ■ Full evidence of links between knowledge and understanding to the application of knowledge and understanding in different contexts (AO2). ■ Detailed, highly relevant and appropriate knowledge and understanding of place(s) and environments used throughout (AO1). ■ Full and accurate knowledge and understanding of key concepts and processes throughout (AO1). ■ Detailed awareness of scale and temporal change, which is well integrated where appropriate (AO1).
Level 3 (11–15 marks)	■ Clear evaluative conclusion that is based on knowledge and understanding, which is applied to the context of the question (AO2). ■ Generally clear, coherent and relevant analysis and evaluation in the application of knowledge and understanding (AO2). ■ Generally clear evidence of links between knowledge and understanding to the application of knowledge and understanding in different contexts (AO2). ■ Generally clear and relevant knowledge and understanding of place(s) and environments (AO1). ■ Generally clear and accurate knowledge and understanding of key concepts and processes (AO1). ■ Generally clear awareness of scale and temporal change, which is integrated where appropriate (AO1).

Level 2 (6–10 marks)	■ Some sense of an evaluative conclusion partially based upon knowledge and understanding, which is applied to the context of the question (AO2). ■ Some partially relevant analysis and evaluation in the application of knowledge and understanding (AO2). ■ Some evidence of links between knowledge and understanding to the application of knowledge and understanding in different contexts (AO2). ■ Some relevant knowledge and understanding of place(s) and environments which is partially relevant (AO1). ■ Some knowledge and understanding of key concepts and processes (AO1). ■ Some awareness of scale and temporal change, which is sometimes integrated where appropriate. There may be a few inaccuracies (AO1).
Level 1 (1–5 marks)	■ Very limited and/or unsupported evaluative conclusion that is loosely based upon knowledge and understanding, which is applied to the context of the question (AO2). ■ Very limited analysis and evaluation in the application of knowledge and understanding. This lacks clarity and coherence (AO2). ■ Very limited and rarely logical evidence of links between knowledge and understanding to the application of knowledge and understanding in different contexts (AO2). ■ Very limited relevant knowledge and understanding of place(s) and environments (AO1). ■ Isolated knowledge and understanding of key concepts and processes (AO1). ■ Very limited awareness of scale and temporal change, which is rarely integrated where appropriate. There may be a number of inaccuracies (AO1).
Level 0 (0 marks)	■ Nothing worthy of credit.

Examination skills

Command words used in the examinations

Command words are the words and phrases used in exams and other assessment tasks that tell students how they should answer the question. The following high level command words could be used:

Analyse Break down concepts, information and/or issues to convey an understanding of them by finding connections and causes, and/or effects.

Assess Consider several options or arguments and weigh them up so as to come to a conclusion about their effectiveness or validity.

Compare Describe the similarities and differences of at least two phenomena.

Evaluate Consider several options, ideas or arguments and form a view based on evidence about their importance/validity/merit/utility.

Examine Consider carefully and provide a detailed account of the indicated topic.

Explain/Why/Suggest reasons for Set out the causes of a phenomenon and/or the factors that influence its form/nature. This usually requires an understanding of processes.

Interpret Ascribe meaning to geographical information and issues.

To what extent Form and express a view as to the merit or validity of a view or statement after examining the evidence available and/or different sides of an argument.

■AS questions

Hazards

Examples of multiple-choice questions

Question 1

What is the name of the place where an earthquake originates beneath the
surface of the Earth?   (1 mark)

A   The epicentre

B   The fracture

C   The focus

D   The seismic point

Question 2

Which scale is most commonly used today to measure earthquakes?   (1 mark)

A   The Mercalli scale

B   The Richter scale

C   The moment magnitude scale

D   The Saffir–Simpson hurricane wind scale

Question 3

What sea temperature is needed for tropical cyclones to form?   (1 mark)

A   20.5°C

B   22.5°C

C   24.5°C

D   27.5°C

Question 4

Most tropical cyclones form between which latitudes?   (1 mark)

A   From the equator to 10°N and 10°S

B   From 5 to 10°N and 5 to 10°S

C   From the equator to 20°N and 20°S

D   From 10 to 15°N and 10 to 15°S

Question 5

When some tsunamis approach the coast, the sea appears to retreat, exposing the seabed before the first wave arrives. What is this phenomenon called?   (1 mark)

A   Backwash

B   Swash

C   Wave retreat

D   Drawback

Answers to multiple-choice questions

Question 1

Correct answer C.   (1 mark)

Question 2

Correct answer C.   (1 mark)

Question 3

Correct answer D.   (1 mark)

Question 4

Correct answer B.   (1 mark)

Question 5

Correct answer D.   (1 mark)

Written-answer questions

Question 1

Outline the basic requirements for wildfires.   (3 marks)

e Mark scheme: 1 mark per valid point.

Student answer

For a wildfire to be created there needs to be two things: an ignition source and a fuel **a**. The former can be caused by lightning during an electrical storm **b**. Another cause of this is human carelessness, such as a discarded cigarette or a badly managed campfire **c**. The main fuel is timber in the form of trees. However, the initial fuel is often dry undergrowth, which can easily catch fire **d**.

e **3/3 marks awarded**. **a b c d** The student provides several valid statements. Maximum credit is awarded.

Question 2

Figures 1a and 1b show information relating to Japan and the Tohoku earthquake 2011. Describe the tectonic setting shown in Figure 1a and link the intensity of the Tohoku earthquake shown in Figure 1b to that setting.

(6 marks)

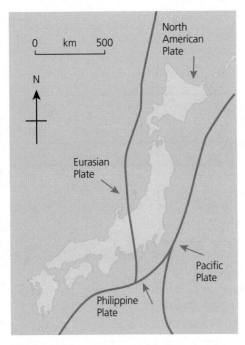

Figure 1a The plate tectonic setting of Japan

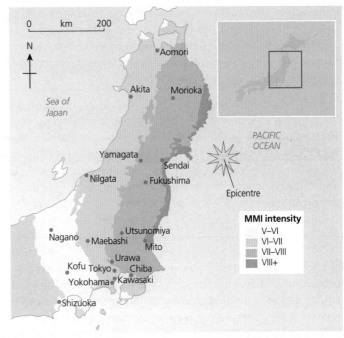

Figure 1b Estimated shaking intensity, Tohoku earthquake (2011)

ⓔ Mark scheme:

- Level 2 (4–6 marks): AO3 — clear use of Figure 1a to describe the tectonic setting, detailed characteristics such as plates, directions of movement and likely landforms/processes. Clear linkage to intensity of earthquake shown in Figure 1b. For full marks, description and linkages should be integrated.
- Level 1 (1–3 marks): AO3 — Basic description of Figure 1a, likely to be simple statements. Reference to linkage to earthquake intensity shown in Figure 1b is basic or absent.

Student answer

Japan sits on two continental plates — the northern part of the country lies on the North American Plate, while the south is on the Eurasian Plate. To the east of Japan are two oceanic plates — in the north is the Pacific Plate, and to the south lies the Philippine Plate. The two oceanic plates are both moving in a generally westward direction at a rate of a few centimetres per year. The zones at which the plates collide lie on the seabed to the east of Japan (Figure 1a) and are marked by deep ocean trenches. At this point the oceanic plates are being forced under the continental plates (known as subduction) and earthquakes take place along such a tectonic boundary **a**.

The earthquake off Sendai in Tohoku in 2011 occurred on the fault that marks the boundary between the Pacific Plate to the east and the North American Plate to the west — 130 km to the east of the port of Sendai. The impact of the earthquake, as measured by the MMI scale on Figure 1b, was greatest all along the 400 km east coastline of Tohoku in a thin band parallel to the coast, north and south of Sendai. The intensity then reduced inland and to the west in a fairly uniform manner, and it also decreased to the southwest. There is, therefore, a strong relation of the intensity of the earthquake to the tectonic setting **b**.

e **5/6 marks awarded.** **a** The student begins with an excellent description of the tectonic setting, making use of both plate names and directions of movement, and making sensible suggestions of both landforms and processes. The background to the earthquake is therefore well explained. The second paragraph then moves on to the second part of the question — linkage to the intensity of the earthquake — by describing the pattern of earthquake intensity. **b** The final sentence makes clear the link that exists, and therefore the answer is integrated. It is a pity that the student did not explore some of the complexities of the relationship, perhaps by commenting on the linear shape of the pattern of intensity. Mid-Level 2 awarded.

Question 3

(Note how this question makes links between two separate areas of the specification, Hazards and Global governance.)

Assess the importance of governance in the successful management of tectonic hazards.

(9 marks)

e Mark scheme:

■ Level 3 (7–9 marks):

– AO1: demonstrates detailed knowledge and understanding of concepts, processes, interactions and change. These underpin the response throughout.

– AO2: applies knowledge and understanding appropriately and with detail. Detailed evidence of the drawing together of a range of geographical ideas, which is used constructively to support the response. Assessment is detailed and well supported with appropriate evidence. A well-balanced and coherent argument is presented.

- Level 2 (4–6 marks):
  - AO1: demonstrates some appropriate knowledge and understanding of concepts, processes, interactions and change. These are mostly relevant although there may be some minor inaccuracy.
  - AO2: applies some knowledge and understanding appropriately. Emerging evidence of the drawing together of a range of geographical ideas, which is used to support the response. Assessment is clear with some support of evidence. A clear argument is presented.
- Level 1 (1–3 marks):
  - AO1: demonstrates basic/limited knowledge and understanding of concepts, processes, interactions and change. These offer limited relevance and/or there is some inaccuracy.
  - AO2: applies limited knowledge and understanding appropriately. Basic evidence of drawing together of a range of geographical ideas, which is used at a basic level to support the response. Assessment is basic, with limited support of evidence. A basic argument is presented.

Student answer

Governance is a vital element in the management of tectonic hazards, and this can take place in a variety of forms: before the event in terms of prediction and preparation, and after the event in terms of relief, rebuilding and rehabilitation [a]. However, extreme events are likely to pose serious challenges for any governance, however well planned. For example, as the 2011 Japanese tsunami illustrated, extreme events are by their nature unpredictable (a one in a 1,000-year event) and so prediction is difficult and prevention is impossible [b]. Also, sometimes secondary and tertiary outcomes occur. In the above example the nuclear power station at Fukushima went into a partial meltdown and valuable resources, money and troops had to be diverted there [c].

Disaster management, before, during and after the event, can have a significant impact on losses, both economic and in terms of deaths. It could be argued that strong governance by the Japanese government before the 2011 tsunami led to significantly fewer deaths (about 19,000) compared with a similar event 7 years earlier: the Indian Ocean Boxing Day tsunami, which caused over 220,000 deaths [d].

Strong governance can lead to very effective management of immediate disaster recovery, as was the case in the Sichuan earthquake in China, where thousands of troops were drafted into the area to assist with the rescue within hours, and they also got involved in dealing with the secondary hazards of landslides and the creation of dammed lakes, which could have overflowed and made the situation even worse. Excellent organisation on the part of the Chinese government made this possible [e]. In the longer term, the Chinese government created long-term education and community preparation strategies should another event occur.

However, it has to be acknowledged that disaster management is expensive and with long return intervals of tectonic hazards, there are strains on budgets that may affect levels of investment. San Francisco has invested lots of money in preparing for the 'big one', by earthquake-proofing many buildings, which some may argue is not cost-effective if the hazard does not actually take place [f].

Another main issue, though, is one of development. The devastating aftermath of the earthquake that took place in Haiti in 2010 illustrated that the country did not have sufficient governance in place before the event, and when many local officials were killed by the earthquake [g], all forms of response become highly ineffective, and it took a very long time for order to be restored.

Governance is highly important in the successful management of tectonic hazards, but it has limitations such as the affordability of prediction and prevention measures, especially in the management of very large hazard events immediately after their occurrence [h].

[e] **9/9 marks awarded.** [a] The student addresses the question at the outset by making a clear statement of assessment. [b] This is then followed by a number of qualifying statements that illustrate a deeper understanding of the task. [c] [d] [e] [f] [g] In each case, and throughout the answer, the student makes good use of exemplar material to support the points being made. The theme of assessment of governance is consistently applied throughout the answer, with a range of case study material used. [h] The answer ends with a clear statement of assessment in the conclusion. Maximum credit awarded.

Question 4

'There is no realistic defence against tropical storms wherever they occur.' To what extent do you agree with this view?   (20 marks)

[e] **Mark scheme: see generic extended response mark scheme on pages 57–58.**

Student answer

Storm events are damaging wherever they occur. These days there are effective satellite monitoring systems to track the development and movement of storms, but they are unable to prevent them occurring or indeed creating havoc. All of these warning systems purely serve to tell people in advance that a storm is coming and to make preparations for when they arrive. Whether or not there can be a realistic defence for storms can be examined in the context of two examples taken from a variety of locations around the world — Hurricane Sandy and Cyclone Nargis [a].

Hurricane Sandy was a tropical cyclone that developed into a hurricane in October 2012 — some called it a 'superstorm' — which moved out of the Caribbean to impact as an extra-tropical storm. In its wake it affected seven countries, which are a mix of developed countries (the USA) and developing countries (such as Jamaica). The effects of Hurricane Sandy varied in these countries on account of a number of factors, including wind strength, storm surge, quality of housing and infrastructure, proximity to the eye of the hurricane and population density b.

Before Sandy reached the USA it had wreaked havoc in the Caribbean. In Jamaica, 70% of the population were left without electricity due to the strong winds and in Haiti, over 100 people were killed and 200,000 left homeless. As the storm passed through Cuba, extensive flooding and strong winds destroyed 15,000 homes and killed 11 people. There was no defence against these events, despite prior warnings c.

In the USA, at least 131 people in eight states were killed. The worst-affected states were New York, New Jersey, Pennsylvania and Maryland. Economic losses due to damage and business interruption were estimated at US$65 billion, making it the second costliest hurricane ever. It affected the entire eastern seaboard from Florida to Maine and west across to Michigan. Damage was particularly severe in New Jersey and New York. Over 8 million people were without power, though the poor quality of the USA's ageing electricity infrastructure was also partly to blame. Residents living on barrier islands in New Jersey were forced to evacuate their homes and some basement dwellers and ground-level residents were forced to evacuate from Hoboken, New Jersey. Over 70 evacuation shelters were opened in New York and all of its airports were closed. The East River overflowed its banks, flooding large areas of Lower Manhattan, including some road tunnels and subway stations. It was reported that the city had a storm surge of almost 3 m and over 100,000 homes on Long Island were damaged or destroyed. Despite New York's wealth and the prior warning that the region was given, it is clear that there were no realistic defences to the forces of Sandy d.

There were wider consequences too. The US Stock Exchange was closed for two days, the first two-day weather closure since 1888. An added complication was that the storm hit the USA just one week before the presidential election. Electioneering was suspended, although President Obama gained favourable television coverage for his empathy with some of the victims. Overall, therefore, the impact of Sandy on one of, if not the, richest countries in the world was devastating. If such a country could not resist such a storm, what chance has any other country e?

Cyclone Nargis hit Burma in April 2008 and caused much damage to the human environment built up around the Irrawaddy delta. The 120 mph winds and 15 ft storm surge swept 15 km inland, destroying homes, farms, boats and lives. Getting statistics was difficult due to the nature of the event and the reluctance of the Burmese government to release the information. However, scientists estimate that 40,000 died and 1 million were left homeless. Severe problems occurred as settlements were situated on riverbanks and coastal areas, as were many farms. This meant that many homes, schools and amenities were destroyed. There was no realistic defence to these. A further long-term problem is that the paddy fields were inundated with seawater, so the soil has become salinized, and so much so that it is now infertile. The cyclone also damaged what little transport infrastructure existed, with bridges, roads and boats being destroyed. This exacerbated the problem, as aid cannot be brought in quickly, and hence a longer term 'defence' was made more difficult f.

These examples serve to illustrate that the statement in the question is correct. All a government can do, assuming they have the financial muscle to afford it, is make preparations to deal with the impacts and aftermaths of storms. They cannot stop them coming — they can just track them coming and prepare. For those countries that do not have the wherewithal to make similar preparations, such as Burma when Cyclone Nargis hit, and Sandy in the Caribbean (as mentioned above), there can be no realistic defence. It is just a case of hoping for the best and doing your best to survive g.

e **19/20 marks awarded.** The response begins with a clear introduction, which sets the scene for what is to follow. a The theme of the question is addressed here at the outset. b The second paragraph then sets the scene for the case study of Hurricane Sandy, which could have been a little shorter, as the factors influencing impacts are not relevant here. c The third paragraph returns to the thrust of the question with some good, detailed case study information. d This is then followed by an impressively detailed paragraph of a range of impacts of Sandy, which is very nicely linked to the question in the final sentence. This is a good example of how learnt facts can be manipulated to meet the needs of a question, but it is crucial that this last part is done. e This is reinforced by the subsequent paragraph, which introduces links to governance and development, together with evidence of critical thinking. The second case study of Cyclone Nargis is not dealt with as thoroughly, f but nevertheless there are also links to governance and food supply (from the option Population and the environment). This is a good technique to employ. There is also a clear link to the question, which is rounded off neatly in the conclusion. g The response also ends with a clear assessment regarding the quotation. It is difficult to fault this answer, though perhaps it could have been slightly more balanced with regards to the case studies. High Level 4 awarded.

■A-level questions

Hazards

Examples of multiple-choice questions

Question 1

What causes the 'storm surge' that often accompanies a cyclone making landfall?   (1 mark)

A   Global warming

B   Low air pressure

C   Intense rainfall

D   Winds pushing waves onshore

Question 2

The Earth's tectonic plates are thought to move across a ductile/plastic layer
above the more solid mantle. What is this layer called?   (1 mark)

A   The lithosphere

B   The core

C   The hydrosphere

D   The asthenosphere

Question 3

In some earthquakes, intense ground shaking causes water-saturated, loose
sediment to behave like a fluid, leading to widespread collapse of structures built
on the sediment. What is this process called?   (1 mark)

A   Liquidisation

B   Liquefaction

C   Solifluction

D   Flooding

Question 4

Tsunami waves are very different from wind-generated ocean waves. Which of
the following correctly describes how tsunami waves are different in the open ocean?   (1 mark)

A   Tsunami waves have longer wavelengths, higher wave heights and travel slower.

B   Tsunami waves have longer wavelengths, smaller wave heights and travel faster.

C   Tsunami waves have shorter wavelengths but higher wave heights.

D   Tsunami waves have longer wavelengths but travel slower.

Question 5

Very large volcanic eruptions can sometimes alter the Earth's climate, usually for a few years only. In what way do they usually alter the climate? (1 mark)

A   Eruptions cause global cooling.

B   Eruptions cause global warming.

C   Eruptions lead to increased rainfall.

D   Eruptions increase hurricane numbers.

Answers to multiple-choice questions

Question 1

Correct answer B. (1 mark)

Question 2

Correct answer D. (1 mark)

Question 3

Correct answer B. (1 mark)

Question 4

Correct answer B. (1 mark)

Question 5

Correct answer A. (1 mark)

Written-answer questions

Question 1

Table 1 The wider impact of the Tohoku tsunami (2011)

Location	Distance from earthquake epicentre (km)	Travel time for tsunami (to nearest hour)	Maximum tsunami wave height on arrival (m)
Scott Base, Antarctica	13,000	22	0.05
NE Tasmania, Australia	9,000	15	0.47
Vancouver Island, Canada	7,200	10	0.79
Valparaiso, Chile	16,900	22	1.54
Santa Cruz, Galapagos Islands	13,200	18	2.26
Fiji	7,300	10	0.21
Tahiti	9,400	11	0.42
North Cape, New Zealand	8,700	12	0.40
Kuril Islands, Kamchatka	1,750	4	2.50
Saipan, Mariana Islands	2,600	3	1.20

Source: USGS

Study Table 1, which shows some aspects of the wider impact of the Tohoku tsunami in 2011. Interpret the information shown. (6 marks)

e Mark scheme:

- **Level 2 (4–6 marks):** AO3 — clear analysis and interpretation of the quantitative evidence provided, which makes appropriate use of data in support. Clear connection(s) between different aspects of the data and geographical evidence.

- **Level 1 (1–3 marks):** AO3 — basic analysis and interpretation of the quantitative evidence provided, which makes limited use of data in support. Basic connection(s) between different aspects of the data and geographical evidence.

Student answer

At first glance it appears that as distance increased from the Tohoku earthquake, the height of the associated tsunami wave decreased, and the travel time increased. These relationships are shown by reference to the Kuril Islands (nearest, short travel time (4 hours) and high wave (2.5 m)) and Scott Base Antarctica (one of the furthest, longest travel times (22 hours) and low wave height (0.05 m)) [a]. However the relationship is not entirely clear. For example, Valparaiso is the furthest by almost 4,000 km, over in South America, and yet the wave reached there at the same time as Scott Base. It also had the third-highest tsunami wave. This could be due to the fact that the wave was pushed along by prevailing winds, such as Trade winds, which would have also maintained the wave's height across the Pacific Ocean [b]. This is reinforced by the fact that Santa Cruz in the Galapagos Islands also had the second-highest wave, at a distance of just over 13,000 km. This wave was only 24 cm smaller than the wave that hit the Kuril Islands, which are 11,000 km nearer to the epicentre [c]. There are some other interesting anomalies, such as Fiji, which had a very low wave height. It is also in the Pacific Ocean, and is half the distance of Santa Cruz. There must be some other factors involved here, such as ocean currents absorbing some of the power perhaps [d].

e 6/6 marks awarded. The student recognises that the data is fairly complex and although some connections can be seen, they are not that simple. [a] The basic relationships within the data are summarised well at first. [b][c][d] He/she then moves on to examine a number of anomalous situations, and seeks to explain them (demonstrating connections with geographical evidence). There is also good use of qualitative and quantitative statements. High Level 2 awarded.

Question 2

Assess the impact of one tropical revolving storm you have studied. (9 marks)

e Mark scheme:

- **Level 3 (7–9 marks):**
  - AO1: demonstrates detailed knowledge and understanding of concepts, processes, interactions and change. These underpin the response throughout.

  - AO2: applies knowledge and understanding appropriately and with detail.
    Detailed evidence of the drawing together of a range of geographical
    ideas, which is used constructively to support the response. Assessment
    is detailed and well supported with appropriate evidence. A well-balanced
    and coherent argument is presented.

■ Level 2 (4–6 marks):

  - AO1: demonstrates some appropriate knowledge and understanding of
    concepts, processes, interactions and change. These are mostly relevant
    although there may be some minor inaccuracy.

  - AO2: applies some knowledge and understanding appropriately. Emerging
    evidence of the drawing together of a range of geographical ideas, which is
    used to support the response. Assessment is clear with some support of
    evidence. A clear argument is presented.

■ Level 1 (1–3 marks):

  - AO1: demonstrates basic/limited knowledge and understanding of
    concepts, processes, interactions and change. These offer limited
    relevance and/or there is some inaccuracy.

  - AO2: applies limited knowledge and understanding appropriately. Basic
    evidence of drawing together of a range of geographical ideas, which is
    used at a basic level to support the response. Assessment is basic with
    limited support of evidence. A basic argument is presented.

Student answer

Typhoon Haiyan was a huge cyclone. It made landfall on 7 November 2013, with
275 km/h sustained wind speeds, a 5 m storm surge and ferocious destructive
power. Up to 290 mm of rainfall fell in 12 hours in some areas. It may have been
the most powerful tropical cyclone ever to make landfall [a]. As Haiyan swept
across the Philippines, it affected upwards of 11 million people, may have killed
as many as 6,300 (which made it the deadliest within the Philippines) and made
hundreds of thousands homeless [b].

The cyclone caused catastrophic destruction, particularly on the islands of
Samar and Leyte, where urban areas were largely destroyed [c]. According to the
UN, about 11 million people were affected and many thousands left homeless.
The actual death toll (around 6,000) remains unclear, with many thousands
of people also declared missing. In Tacloban City the terminal building at the
airport was destroyed by a 5.2 m-high storm surge.

Guiuan, a fishing town in Eastern Samar, was the point of Haiyan's first landfall,
and was severely affected by the typhoon's impacts. Nearly all structures in the
town suffered at least partial damage, many of which were completely flattened.
For several days following Haiyan's first landfall the damage situation remained
unclear due to lack of communication [d]. There was widespread devastation
from the storm surge in Tacloban City, especially in San Jose, with many
buildings being destroyed, trees knocked over or broken, and cars piled up. The
low-lying areas on the eastern side of Tacloban City were hardest hit, with some
areas completely washed away. Flooding also extended for 1 km inland on the
east coast. It was estimated that roughly 90% of the city had been destroyed [e].

Large parts of Leyte and Samar were without power for up to a month afterwards. Trees blocked major roads, making them impassable. Around 450 domestic and international airline flights were cancelled [j]. Some airports in the region were also closed on November 8 and 9, and ferries were affected. Relief and rescue efforts were underway by 9 November, but some places remained isolated and out of communication due to severe damage for several days afterwards [g]. Throughout Tacloban City, widespread looting took place in the days following Haiyan's passage. In some instances, relief trucks were attacked and had food stolen in the city. Two of the city's shopping malls and numerous grocery stores were subjected to looting. Security checkpoints were set up all over Tacloban and a curfew was imposed on residents to prevent more attacks. Looting intensified as slow recovery efforts forced residents to seek any means necessary to survive [h]. Further complicating efforts to retain order was the lack of officers reporting for work. In Tacloban, only 100 of the city's 1,300 police personnel reported for duty.

(e) **7/9 marks awarded**. This is a highly detailed account of one tropical storm event. [a] [b] [c] [e] [f] As well as giving accurate details of the impact, the student provides a number of instances of explicit assessment of impact. [d] [g] [h] Furthermore, there are a few occasions where the student provides commentary on the impacts, which is evidence of application of knowledge. The main weakness is that there is no overall assessment of relative impact of, say, social vs economic vs environmental vs political. Low Level 3 awarded.

Question 3

(Note how this question makes links between two separate areas of the specification, Hazards and Changing places.)

Examine how volcanoes can influence people's emotional attachment to a place. (9 marks)

(e) Mark scheme:

■ Level 3 (7–9 marks):
- AO1: demonstrates detailed knowledge and understanding of concepts, processes, interactions and change. These underpin the response throughout.
- AO2: applies knowledge and understanding appropriately and with detail. Detailed evidence of the drawing together of a range of geographical ideas, which is used constructively to support the response. Analysis is detailed and well supported with appropriate evidence. A well-balanced and coherent argument is presented.

■ Level 2 (4–6 marks):
- AO1: demonstrates some appropriate knowledge and understanding of concepts, processes, interactions and change. These are mostly relevant although there may be some minor inaccuracy.
- AO2: applies some knowledge and understanding appropriately. Emerging evidence of the drawing together of a range of geographical ideas, which is used to support the response. Analysis is clear with some support of evidence. A clear argument is presented.

- **Level 1 (1–3 marks):**
  - AO1: demonstrates basic/limited knowledge and understanding of concepts, processes, interactions and change. These offer limited relevance and/or there is some inaccuracy.
  - AO2: applies limited knowledge and understanding appropriately. Basic evidence of drawing together of a range of geographical ideas, which is used at a basic level to support the response. Analysis is basic with limited support of evidence. A basic argument is presented.

Student answer

Volcanoes and volcanic eruptions can influence emotional attachment to place according to the degree of risk posed by the volcano. This could then be conveyed between several generations to influence an individual's and a community's perception, and hence emotional attachment. For example, many remote communities in Asia attach a lot of cultural significance to living near a volcano — it is part of their community and identity a.

Volcanic eruptions have influenced people's activities in the area of Naples, around Mt Vesuvius. Two large eruptions thousands of years ago left thick deposits of tephra, which have weathered to form rich, fertile soils. This area is abundant for farming and there are a number of tourist-related economic activities. These include the famous tourist site of Pompeii, which owes its existence to a volcanic event. The Roman city was buried by an eruption and it has subsequently been rediscovered, and so it is a very popular tourist attraction and many people depend on it economically. Attachment is therefore strong b.

Elsewhere, Iceland utilises its tectonic and volcanic activity for economic gain through tourism and geothermal energy, and it is very much a part of the country's identity. The geothermal energy and tourism (geysers, volcanoes, geothermal spas) are very much part of people's daily lives and their way of supporting themselves, producing food (greenhouses) and a source of revenue (tours, hotels etc.). Therefore their emotional attachment to their place is very strong c.

The perception of a volcanic eruption depends on the probability of it happening, the scale of the event and technological advancement to mitigate against the risk. Despite Montserrat last erupting in 1995, the inhabitants from the south of the island still no longer live there as they were evacuated off the island or to the north. Despite people's emotional attachment to their place, a strong fishing community and tourism industry, the continued eruptions have made it too risky to return home and there has been very little clean up. The perception of risk before 1995 was low, as the previous eruption was 300 years ago, and yet the long-term effects of the recent eruption have been devastating on individuals and the community of Montserrat d.

ⓔ 9/9 marks awarded. This answer is conceptually strong in that some of the theory of Changing place studies is transferred across to this option, rather than the other way around. **ⓐ** The opening paragraph is conceptually strong and sets the scene for what is to follow. **ⓑ ⓒ** The second and third paragraphs relate these ideas to two examples, which are both detailed and accurate, and linked to the question. **ⓓ** The final paragraph provides a further sophisticated example, which neatly connects to the introduction through the theme of risk. A well-constructed answer that always keeps the focus of the question to the fore. High Level 3 awarded.

Question 4

'The hazards presented by volcanic and seismic events have the greatest impact on the world's poorest people.' To what extent do you agree with this view?   (20 marks)

ⓔ Mark scheme: see generic extended response mark scheme on pages 57-58.

Student answer

Tectonic hazards such as earthquakes and volcanic eruptions occur across the surface of the globe, and many argue that they have the greatest impact on the poorest people — the inhabitants of developing countries. However, there are several other different factors, such as magnitude and location, which contribute to the severity of a tectonic event, both physical and human **ⓐ**.

First, I do not agree with this view because the severity of an event and the impact it has obviously depends on the magnitude of the event. For example, the Banda Aceh earthquake of 26 December 2004 off the coast of Indonesia measured 9.1 on the Richter scale, whereas L'Aquila earthquake in Abruzzo, Italy, in 2009 only measured 6.3 on the Richter scale. Volcanic eruptions also differ in explosivity. Mt Etna on Sicily erupted in 2008 with only Strombolian activity, whereas the 1995–97 Soufrière Hills eruptions on Montserrat varied from Pelean to Plinean activity — much more explosive **ⓑ**.

Second, the type of event also determines the impact it has on people, both rich and poor. With the L'Aquila earthquake, the only primary effect it produced was ground shaking for 20 seconds, whereas the Banda Aceh earthquake was submarine and it produced tsunami waves. There were several waves varying from 20 m to 30 m in height. This made the tsunami's impact far more widespread, as the waves travelled a great distance across the Indian Ocean, affecting different countries as far apart as South Africa and Indonesia, India and Burma. Volcanic eruptions also come in different forms. Volcanoes found on destructive margins often lie dormant for long periods of time. Then they produce explosive and violent eruptions of acidic lava, pyroclastic flows, ash and larger lava bombs. The eruptions on Montserrat were of this nature. Constructive margins and hotspots produce gentle eruptions of lava, which are more continuous and less threatening **ⓒ**.

These factors, magnitude and type do have a large effect on its impact. However, I mainly agree with the view that aspects of human geography have the greatest impact on whether a tectonic event becomes a 'natural disaster'. And it is true that most of these are dependent on the level of economic development of a country **ⓓ**.

First, the population density of the area, as well as the land use and infrastructure, determines the input of the event. The countries bordering the Indian Ocean are mainly developing nations, with many fishing communities living on the coast. The coastal geography in places like Thailand and Indonesia is low-lying. However, it is also densely populated, often with mainly poorly built houses and poor roads and communications. This contributed to the destruction of the area by the Boxing Day tsunami and made it more difficult for remote communities to receive aid. The same was true for Montserrat: 50% of the water supply network was destroyed by the eruption and the capital Plymouth was covered in ash. However, the lack of roads and communications on other parts of the island made it again difficult to obtain aid. On the other hand, the Italian medieval city of L'Aquila had good communications by road and rail, and although it was built on lake sediments, which amplified the shaking, rescue workers were able to deliver a reasonable level of aid after the earthquake e.

A, or perhaps 'the', major determinant of the impact of a tectonic event is the level of protection, prediction and preparation a country has against tectonic hazards. For example, Japan has an excellent tsunami warning system, which can relay public warnings within three minutes of the seismic event. It has also built tsunami walls to aid tsunami shelters along the coast. As a consequence, a 30 m tsunami that occurred in 2005 killed only 240 people. On the other hand, the Boxing Day tsunami killed an estimated 230,000 people. One of the main reasons for this is that the countries bordering the Indian Ocean are developing countries and so could not at that time afford a warning system. One has subsequently been installed in the Indian Ocean. It should also be pointed out that the tsunami walls did little to protect the east coast of Japan during the Tohoku earthquake and tsunami in March 2011 f.

On the other hand, it is not just developing countries that suffer from poor hazard management. A Californian scientist commented of the L'Aquila earthquake that 'an earthquake of this magnitude in California wouldn't have killed a single person'. The major reason L'Aquila was lethal was because of the collapse of old medieval buildings and more modern buildings with poor workmanship, and poor land-use planning. Italy is a developed country and still suffered considerably g.

The next major difference between developing and developed countries in their response to natural disasters is their own ability to provide relief after the event. In the 2008 Etna eruption, £5.6 million in tax breaks was granted by the government, and in the L'Aquila earthquake, emergency crews were at the scene within minutes and international aid arrived within 24 hours. By contrast, poorer nations are almost completely dependent on foreign aid to respond to tectonic hazards. The foreign aid given for the tsunami was US$7 billion but this pales into insignificance next to the aid given for natural disasters by rich governments when they have occurred in rich countries (e.g. in the aftermath of Hurricane Katrina, US$62.3 billion was provided). In Montserrat, aid took several days to come and when it did, some was inappropriate. The water supply and sewage disposal was also inadequate and so gastrointestinal disease spread. In this way, poorer people in developing countries suffer more from

from earthquakes and eruptions because foreign aid is so often not enough/is substandard h.

Furthermore, people in developing countries generally have fewer possessions — perhaps a few livestock or a fishing boat are the most important. So, when these are lost in a natural disaster they lose more than possessions — they actually lose their livelihoods. For example, during the 2004 tsunami, 60% of Sri Lanka's fishing fleet was destroyed. What is even more damaging is the fact that such countries are dependent on foreign aid to recover, and this is unreliable. The government of Sri Lanka reported six months after the event that it had received no foreign aid. The Soufrière Hills eruption threw the Montserrat economy back into dependency on the UK, just as it had reached a level of independence. One of the reasons for this is that Montserrat is dependent on its primary sector, particularly farming. The volcanic slopes are the most fertile and so provide most of the food supply and exports. When these were covered in ash, the crops failed i.

So, overall, although physical factors have an extremely important role to play, natural volcanic and seismic disasters are often not that, but are in fact 'human-made' disasters. As a consequence, the poorer countries are indeed the ones that suffer the most j.

e **19/20 marks awarded.** a The answer begins with a brief introduction that sets the scene for the essay, and establishes that factors other than poverty may have a bearing. b This is followed by some recognition that the size of the event may be important — which demonstrates that the student is addressing the element of the question 'To what extent...'. c The third paragraph provides clear recognition that the nature of the event plays a role in the impact of tectonic events. Again, this is addressing the 'To what extent...' element of the question.

d Having challenged the statement, the student now moves towards addressing the main thrust of the statement — the roles of relative economic development and poverty. In the next paragraph, the student takes the theme of infrastructure, and points out its importance in both the aftermath and relief operations. Snippets of knowledge and facts are used to reinforce the points being made — they are just sufficient for the task. e Superfluous information is not given — the student is clearly in control of the task. f Warning systems for tsunamis are the focus of the next section, with clear and accurate statements of difference based on development. g The reference to L'Aquila in the next paragraph and the quotation provide interesting counter-views. This is followed by an excellent paragraph on the role of aid, and its organisation. Clear contrasts are given, with detailed specific information. h The reference to Hurricane Katrina may initially appear irrelevant, but it is used to illustrate the point being made — a high level of insight. i Further aspects of the impact on livelihoods and economies are discussed next, again with good use of exemplar material together with valid commentary. j A short conclusion ends the answer, but it does clearly return to the thrust of the task.

The essay is not perfect, yet within the time constraints, it is difficult to imagine a better answer. Its biggest strength is that it addresses the question throughout, and does not give a case-study-by-case-study account. Ideas and themes are assembled in a structured manner and supported throughout by the appropriate use of facts from a very wide range of case studies, which are well integrated. There is strong evidence of critical understanding, with frequent elements of linkage to other aspects of geography. The argument is focused, logical, structured and mature. High Level 4 awarded.

Population and the environment

Examples of multiple-choice questions

Question 1

What type of migrant is outside their home country, and has been granted the right to stay in a country because of fear of violence or persecution? (1 mark)

A   Refugee

B   Internally displaced person

C   Asylum seeker

D   Illegal migrant

Question 2

Salinisation of soils occurs when: (1 mark)

A   Extra manure is added to reduce the salts in the soil

B   Fertilisers are used to add nitrates and phosphates to the soil

C   Rapid drainage leads to salts being leached downwards to the lower horizons of the soil

D   Water is drawn to the surface by excess evaporation and this precipitates salts near to the surface of the soil

Question 3

When a country moves from Stage 4 to Stage 5 of the Demographic Transition Model, the following situation exists: (1 mark)

A   Low birth and death rates but with the death rate lower than the birth rate

B   A high level of immigration, which causes a spike in birth rates

C   Low death and birth rates but with the birth rate lower than the death rate

D   Birth control is widespread causing a further lowering of the birth rate

Question 4

The Population, Resources and Pollution (PRP) model states that: (1 mark)

A Population growth is geometric, resources growth is arithmetic, and hence there will be pollution

B When there are too few people to use the resources of an area, there will be no pollution

C There are several feedback mechanisms between population growth, resource use and pollution

D The resources that are available in an area are developed by the population to produce high living standards but much pollution

Question 5

Which is the correct definition of annual net migration? (1 mark)

A The total number of immigrants a country receives in a year

B The difference between the number of immigrants and emigrants in a year

C The number of emigrants minus the number of children born to immigrants

D The total number of emigrants leaving a country each year

Answers to multiple-choice questions

Question 1

Correct answer A. (1 mark)

Question 2

Correct answer D. (1 mark)

Question 3

Correct answer C. (1 mark)

Question 4

Correct answer C. (1 mark)

Question 5

Correct answer B. (1 mark)

Written-answer questions

Set of questions A

Question 1

Table 2 Human Development Index (HDI) and % of foreign-born residents in selected countries (2014)

Country	Norway	USA	France	Czech Republic	Iran	Egypt	India	Nigeria	Malawi
HDI	0.94	0.91	0.88	0.85	0.75	0.68	0.58	0.50	0.43
% of foreign-born residents	11.8	14.3	11.5	4.0	3.5	0.4	0.4	0.7	1.3

Study Table 2, which shows some aspects of development and population for some selected countries. Interpret the information shown. (6 marks)

ⓔ Mark scheme:

- Level 2 (4–6 marks): AO3 — clear analysis and interpretation of the quantitative evidence provided, which makes appropriate use of data in support. Clear connection(s) between different aspects of the data and geographical evidence.

- Level 1 (1–3 marks): AO3 — basic analysis and interpretation of the quantitative evidence provided, which makes limited use of data in support. Basic connection(s) between different aspects of the data and geographical evidence.

> **Student answer**
>
> The Human Development Index (HDI) includes GDP per capita among the criteria that are used to create it — the higher the HDI, the better the standard of living (and GDP) for the people living in that country. It is clear that richer economies will be more attractive to migrants as they will want to have a higher standard of living, both economic migrants and refugees fleeing persecution. This is shown by the data in Table 2, where three of the four countries with HDI over 0.8 have over 11% foreign-born residents ⓐ. More developed societies such as these are likely to have higher demand for labour, and so have more immigrants seeking work. The countries with low HDI scores, such as Iran and Nigeria, may have autocratic governments or suffer from internal divisions and conflict, which will make them unattractive to immigrants and may indeed accelerate out-migration ⓑ. The slight exception to this is Iran, which has a slightly higher amount of migrants than might be expected. This could be because it is located near to Afghanistan and migrants fleeing the war there may have crossed over the border ⓒ. The Czech Republic is an interesting anomaly in that it has a relatively high HDI, yet a low percentage of foreign-born residents. It is quite a new country, so perhaps it isn't known that well by economic migrants ⓓ.

ⓔ 6/6 marks awarded. The student recognises that the data has some complexity and although some connections can be seen, they are not all straightforward. ⓐ A basic relationship within the data is summarised well at first and ⓑ possible explanations for this (linking to other geographical evidence) are also offered. ⓒ ⓓ He/she then moves on to examine a number of anomalous situations, and seeks to explain them (demonstrating connections with other geographical evidence). There is good use of qualitative and quantitative statements throughout. High Level 2 awarded.

Question 2

Examine how the age-sex composition of a country's population changes at different stages of the Demographic Transition Model.

(9 marks)

ⓔ Mark scheme:

■ **Level 3 (7–9 marks):**

– AO1: demonstrates detailed knowledge and understanding of concepts, processes, interactions and change. These underpin the response throughout.

– AO2: applies knowledge and understanding appropriately and with detail. Detailed evidence of the drawing together of a range of geographical ideas, which is used constructively to support the response. Analysis is detailed and well supported with appropriate evidence. A well-balanced and coherent argument is presented.

■ **Level 2 (4–6 marks):**

– AO1: demonstrates some appropriate knowledge and understanding of concepts, processes, interactions and change. These are mostly relevant although there may be some minor inaccuracy.

– AO2: applies some knowledge and understanding appropriately. Emerging evidence of the drawing together of a range of geographical ideas, which is used to support the response. Analysis is clear with some support of evidence. A clear argument is presented.

■ **Level 1 (1–3 marks):**

– AO1: demonstrates basic/limited knowledge and understanding of concepts, processes, interactions and change. These offer limited relevance and/or there is some inaccuracy.

– AO2: applies limited knowledge and understanding appropriately. Basic evidence of drawing together of a range of geographical ideas, which is used at a basic level to support the response. Analysis is basic with limited support of evidence. A basic argument is presented.

Student answer

Different population structures of age-sex compositions at different stages of the Demographic Transition Model (DTM) can be shown effectively through the diagrams known as population pyramids. For Stage 1 of the DTM there are high and fluctuating birth and death rates. This gives us a wide base on the population pyramid, indicating a youthful population. Also, the sharply indenting sides show the high death rate and low life expectancy as there is poor healthcare, and technological advances in fighting diseases are non-existent, resulting in few older people. There are few countries at this stage in the world today — perhaps Afghanistan is the closest to it **a**.

In Stage 2 of the DTM, death rates fall while birth rates stay the same. This means that there is a high natural increase, as there are many more people being born than dying. The pyramid shows that there is now a slightly larger elderly population than before, because people now live longer — longer life expectancy as healthcare improves, but mostly because there is better-quality nutrition and better water sanitation systems. Several of the countries of sub-Saharan Africa are thought to fit this pattern, such as Mali and Niger **b**.

As a country progresses to Stage 3 of the DTM, the upper part of the pyramid begins to properly fill out — to widen. There are now many more equal proportions (but not yet equal) between younger and older elements of the population. This is because birth rates have begun to fall due to the introduction of contraception (family planning) and because children begin to become an economic burden. A larger proportion of middle-aged people between 25 and 45 becomes apparent, as well as more elderly. Countries currently at this stage are Brazil, India and Mexico. This 'window' of low economic dependency within the population has been called a 'demographic dividend' but the countries need to have the right level of governance to exploit it **c**.

In Stage 4 we see a very balanced pyramid with largely vertical sides, because both death rates and birth rates are very low and almost equal. Life expectancy is also higher than before, so there are more older people. The UK was in this category until recently, when an increase in birth rates caused by migration has produced a small spike in the base of the pyramid.

Lastly, Stage 5 is believed to be where some countries, such as Germany, Italy and Japan are entering. This is because birth rates could further drop and we would end up with an elderly or ageing population where the majority are over age 60. This is the only stage where there may be a major gender variation, as women tend to live longer than men, so there are more elderly women in this stage **d**.

e **9/9 marks awarded**. This answer follows an approach where each of the DTM stages is examined in turn. The analysis throughout is detailed and sophisticated. **a** The first paragraph describes the shape of the pyramid of Stage 1, with explanation of the processes behind it, and an example. **b** This strategy is continued in the next paragraph. **c** The third paragraph is particularly sophisticated, with a reference to the demographic dividend and governance. **d** The final two paragraphs complete the task, with Stages 4 and 5 of the DTM, with a neat little reference to gender differences at the end. Overall this is a very thorough answer. High Level 3 awarded.

Question 3

(Note how this question makes links between two separate areas of the specification, Population and the environment and Global systems.)

Examine how food security can impact social inequality.   (9 marks)

ⓔ Mark scheme:

- **Level 3 (7–9 marks):**
  - AO1: demonstrates detailed knowledge and understanding of concepts, processes, interactions and change. These underpin the response throughout.
  - AO2: applies knowledge and understanding appropriately and with detail. Detailed evidence of the drawing together of a range of geographical ideas, which is used constructively to support the response. Analysis is detailed and well supported with appropriate evidence. A well-balanced and coherent argument is presented.

- **Level 2 (4–6 marks):**
  - AO1: demonstrates some appropriate knowledge and understanding of concepts, processes, interactions and change. These are mostly relevant although there may be some minor inaccuracy.
  - AO2: applies some knowledge and understanding appropriately. Emerging evidence of the drawing together of a range of geographical ideas, which is used to support the response. Analysis is clear with some support of evidence. A clear argument is presented.

- **Level 1 (1–3 marks):**
  - AO1: demonstrates basic/limited knowledge and understanding of concepts, processes, interactions and change. These offer limited relevance and/or there is some inaccuracy.
  - AO2: applies limited knowledge and understanding appropriately. Basic evidence of drawing together of a range of geographical ideas, which is used at a basic level to support the response. Analysis is basic with limited support of evidence. A basic argument is presented.

Student answer

Food security relates to the ability of all people at all times to have access to sufficient, safe and nutritious food. The concept of social inequality is measured through indices such as housing, healthcare, education, employment and access to services [a]. Spatial patterns of social inequality vary both within and between places, and these can be influenced by structural economic or political change. In Zimbabwe, for example, human and physical factors have combined to cause issues with food security. Here there is often poor weather in the form of drought, which affects harvests, as well as government land reform and agricultural policies, which have made the provision of food in the country worse. Some of the best farmers in the country — the white European farmers — have had their land taken from them. This has contributed to poor levels of food security in the country, with only the wealthy managing to afford to buy food [b].

Access and affordability of food is an issue across the development spectrum. While developing countries traditionally have less access to food and a lack of money to buy food, this can also be evident in developed countries such as the UK, where we are increasingly seeing food banks and soup kitchens in areas of social need. The lack of access to food and it being unaffordable for some is an indicator of social inequality c.

Education is another key factor. There is an ongoing debate about what constitutes a healthy diet. Nutritional requirements for different groups of people vary. For example, children in remote rural areas in developing countries such as Zambia need certain levels of vitamins and protein, whereas in many developed parts of the world, such as the UK, there is a strong focus on excessive salt and sugar content in processed foods, which have a direct impact on medical conditions such as obesity. Foods that are low in nutritional content and high in salt and fat are often low cost and therefore the only affordable option to the lowest income groups d.

While people might be seen to be more food secure in a global sense, the uneven distribution of this resource is clearly linked to social inequality. In the developed world, again the UK, there has been an emphasis recently on organic and some health foods. These are often high cost and therefore unaffordable to disadvantaged sections of society e.

e **9/9 marks awarded**. At first this seems a challenging task and many students may find it difficult understanding how to link the two seemingly quite different areas of the specification. Nevertheless, as with all other such 'linking' examination questions, you have to read and understand the task, and answer it. This answer is conceptually strong throughout but also makes good use of exemplification and detail. a The answer begins with a clarification of the two terms in the question. b This is followed by an example that addresses the causes of food insecurity in Zimbabwe but then links it to social inequality. c d e The second, third and fourth paragraphs then provide some interesting links between food security and inequality in relation to the UK — food banks, obesity and organic foods — each of which demonstrate excellent application of knowledge and understanding. Some sophisticated points are being made here — the sign of a strong candidate. High Level 3 awarded.

Question 4

'Infectious diseases have a greater impact on economic development than non-communicable diseases.' To what extent do you agree with this view?

(20 marks)

e Mark scheme: see generic extended response mark scheme on pages 57–58.

Student answer

Some would agree with this statement, because seemingly infectious diseases can be spread easily from person to person and so if they are not controlled, they can affect large proportions of a population quickly and therefore have a great impact on economic development. In recent years, the rapid spread of Ebola in West Africa has caused turmoil in the countries there. There were major social impacts and severe economic impacts, not only for the countries affected but also for the countries that provided the emergency healthcare that was needed. Rapidly deployed doctors, nurses, hospitals, drugs and equipment all had to be paid for by someone. Hence the economic impact of any disease can be said to be great. To examine this in more detail, this essay will concentrate on the economic impact of two diseases: malaria, an infectious disease, and cancer, a non-communicable disease [a].

Malaria has serious and far-reaching impacts, slowing economic growth and development, and prolonging the vicious cycle of poverty that exists in many developing countries, especially in sub-Saharan Africa. While it is true that poverty and lack of development may be a key cause of the presence of malaria, there is a strong argument that malaria causes further underdevelopment.

There are several costs involved, both to individuals and governments. Costs to individuals and their families include the purchase of drugs for treating malaria, expenses for travel to (and treatment at) clinics, lost days of work, reduction in crop production, absence from school, expenses for preventive measures and ultimately burial in the tragic situation of death. Costs to governments include maintenance, supply and staffing of health facilities, the purchase of drugs and supplies, public health interventions against malaria (such as insecticide spraying or distribution of insecticide-treated bed nets), lost days of work with resulting loss of income, and lost opportunities for major economic ventures and tourism [b].

It has been estimated that in some parts of sub-Saharan Africa, malaria accounts for up to 40% of public health expenditures (involving mosquito control, education and research), 50% of inpatient hospital admissions and 60% of outpatient health clinic visits. Direct costs (for example, illness, treatment and premature death) have been estimated to be at least US$12 billion per year. The cost in lost economic growth is many times more than that, and is impossible to measure [c].

In terms of impact, malaria is the biggest killer of all parasitic diseases. Economically it accounts for millions of working days lost, and there are high costs of treatment, both for individuals and countries. The World Health Organization (WHO) estimates that malaria can decrease the GDP of a country by as much as 1.3% in countries with high disease rates. It disrupts schooling through absenteeism, and creates nutrition deficiencies and anaemia in women in malarial regions. As a result, 25% of first babies in some areas have a low birth weight, and their ongoing care will have a long-term economic impact. So, for many poorer countries, infectious diseases such as malaria have worse economic impacts, because they already do not have the funds or resources to effectively manage the disease [d].

Cancer is a non-communicable disease — it cannot be caught by transmission. It is also known as a disease of affluence, so is mainly found in developed countries. It is expected to kill over 20 million a year by 2030. Its rise is thought to be caused by a result of the misuse of alcohol and tobacco, poor diet (not enough fruit and vegetables), and it has also been shown that there is a strong correlation between age and infection. The older you are the more likely you are to be affected by cancer in some form [e].

In terms of personal health and economics, it can prevent you from working, as treatment is often long and painful, and involves the use of drugs and radiology. This means that you will suffer a loss of income. In economic terms, the loss of working time will have a negative effect on the economy. It has been shown that smoking costs the world economy US$200 billion a year and inactivity in work costs the US economy US$25 billion a year. These both have a direct link to cancer, so this shows the sheer cost that each factor has to the economy. Also, it is likely that sufferers of cancer will be looked after by relatives who are of working age, so this also means they will be losing an income and affecting the economy. In addition, all treatment for cancer is aimed at reducing pain and not curing, as no direct cure has been found yet. This shows the severe longer-term economic impacts cancer has. More research is needed so that a cure can be developed, as well as better methods of detection, so it can be caught earlier f.

Comparing the two types of disease, NCDs are usually age related and so are more likely to occur in later life. On the other hand, infectious diseases can affect anyone and so even children can die from them. This means that infectious diseases cause a greater loss of the workforce, as high infant mortality rates mean that children will not grow up and join the workforce. Therefore, infectious diseases slow economic growth in the long term more than NCDs. On the other hand, people with an infectious disease may recover quickly if they are treated and so the overall loss to productivity will be low in this scenario. People with an NCD, such as CHD, may suffer from angina and lethargy for many years and so productivity losses are large g.

The effect on economic development also depends on which country is studied. In richer countries, such as the UK, most infectious diseases are treated easily and are prevented through vaccinations. Problems arise, however, when people return to the country, say from holiday, with a rare form of infectious disease. One of the nurses who treated Ebola patients in Sierra Leone came back with the disease, and her treatment involved a lot of costs, but without impacting on the UK's economic development. NCDs are more common in the UK but healthcare is available to treat the symptoms. In contrast to this, a poorer country may suffer more from an infectious disease or may increasingly suffer from NCDs, too, due to changing lifestyles as they become more Westernised. However, healthcare here is less readily available and the relative cost of treatment is much higher because the country is much poorer. Therefore I think that an overall assessment of the quotation in the question is more complex — for a developed country an NCD has the greatest impact on economic development and for a developing country an infectious disease has the greatest impact h.

e **19/20 marks awarded.** This is a coherent, analytical and sophisticated answer. a It begins with a clear introduction, and although the student states that he/she will concentrate on two identified diseases, a brief overview of a third, Ebola, is offered. b c The subsequent paragraphs provide a sophisticated summary of the economic impacts of malaria on individuals and governments, which ends with some impressive statistics that seem plausible, though perhaps impossible to verify. d Further analysis of economic impacts of malaria follows — perhaps slightly repetitive of previous points but nevertheless perceptive. The answer then considers the impact of cancer in general. Perhaps it might have been better to concentrate on one form of the condition, but that might not have been the decision of the student — the teacher could have chosen to study 'cancer' in general. e f Although not quite at the same level or as detailed as the discussion on malaria, some interesting and valid points are made. g The student then begins to compare the economic impact of the two types of disease considered and some good discursive points are made. The concluding paragraph continues an evaluative approach, and somewhat cleverly returns to Ebola. h A clear overall view with regard to the statement in the question is provided, demonstrating some complexity of thought, rounding off the answer neatly. This is a good answer for a challenging task. High Level 4 awarded.

Set of questions B

Question 1

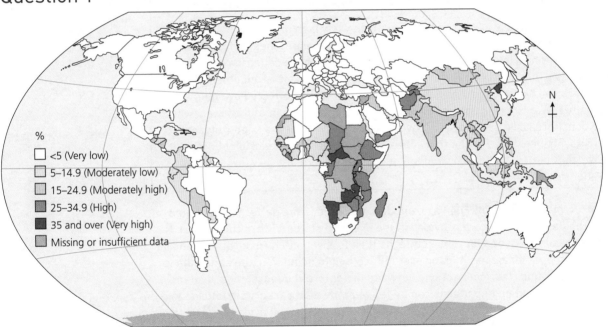

Figure 2 Global prevalence of undernourishment (%), 2014–16

**Study Figure 2, which shows the global prevalence of undernourishment.
Interpret the information shown.**

(6 marks)

e Mark scheme:

■ Level 2 (4–6 marks): AO3 — clear analysis and interpretation of the qualitative and quantitative evidence provided, which makes appropriate use of data in support. Clear recognition of patterns within the data. Clear connection(s) between different aspects of the data and geographical evidence.

■ **Level 1 (1–3 marks): AO3** — basic analysis and interpretation of the qualitative and quantitative evidence provided, which makes limited use of data in support. Basic/limited recognition of patterns within the data. Basic connection(s) between different aspects of the data and geographical evidence.

Student answer

Figure 2 shows that the main area of prevalence of undernourishment is in sub-Saharan Africa, with countries such as Namibia and Zambia having very high levels of undernourishment in the population, over 35% **a**. Other countries in this region of the world have high levels of undernourishment, particularly along the eastern side of Africa — places like Ethiopia and Tanzania **b**. All of these countries have low food security due to unreliable rainfall in their climates, population pressures and lack of development. Here, a large proportion of the farmers remain subsistence, and the land that is given over to commercial farming is used for cash crops for the developing world such as cotton, tobacco and even roses (grown in Ethiopia for western European supermarket shelves). As a result, there is less grown for food and nutrition levels fall **c**.

Elsewhere there are areas of high and moderately high undernourishment in Latin America (Bolivia) and Asia (Afghanistan, India and Yemen) **d**. North Korea has a very high level of undernourishment. Many of these countries have similar issues as the African countries — poor rainfall and lack of development — but others, such as Afghanistan and North Korea, are being affected by political factors. War and civil unrest has affected food production in Afghanistan, while North Korea has an oppressive government that controls the supply of food to its inhabitants **e**. For the rest of the world, the developed world of Europe, North America, Australasia and the middle east, there are very low levels of undernourishment **f**.

---

e **6/6 marks awarded**. **a b** The candidate recognises the patterns illustrated by the data and these are provided in the first two statements of the answer. **c** The possible reasons for these patterns then follow, initially in a rather general manner, but then by use of good exemplification. In doing this, the candidate is demonstrating clear connections between the data and geographical evidence. **d** More recognition of patterns can be found in the next paragraph, followed again by clear connections to other aspects of geographical evidence, **e**, in this case governance. **f** The answer ends with another statement of pattern. High Level 2 awarded.

Question 2

Assess two strategies that have led to an increase in food production.   (9 marks)

🄮 Mark scheme:

- Level 3 (7–9 marks):
  - AO1: demonstrates detailed and balanced knowledge and understanding of concepts, processes, interactions and change. These underpin the response throughout.
  - AO2: applies knowledge and understanding appropriately and with detail. Detailed evidence of the drawing together of a range of geographical ideas, which is used constructively to support the response. Assessment is detailed and well supported with appropriate evidence. A well-balanced and coherent argument is presented.
- Level 2 (4–6 marks):
  - AO1: demonstrates some appropriate knowledge and understanding of concepts, processes, interactions and change, which may be imbalanced. These are mostly relevant although there may be some minor inaccuracy.
  - AO2: applies some knowledge and understanding appropriately. Emerging evidence of the drawing together of a range of geographical ideas, which is used to support the response. Assessment is clear with some support of evidence. A clear argument is presented.
- Level 1 (1–3 marks):
  - AO1: demonstrates basic/limited knowledge and understanding of concepts, processes, interactions and change. These offer limited relevance and/or there is some inaccuracy.
  - AO2: applies limited knowledge and understanding appropriately. Basic evidence of drawing together of a range of geographical ideas, which is used at a basic level to support the response. Assessment is basic with limited support of evidence. A basic argument is presented.

Student answer

The Green Revolution was first developed in Mexico in the 1950s and 1960s. It was then introduced in India in 1960, where it was most successful. The aim was to boost food production using irrigation, fertiliser, pesticides and high-yielding varieties (HYVs) of seeds. It also used mechanisation 🄰. Buffaloes were replaced by tractors and fertilisers, and pesticides were used to allow double cropping and to prevent insects killing crops. The use of fertilisers meant that crops would grow fast, helping to feed the ever-expanding population in the country. HYVs have also helped to increase food production, as crops such as wheat/rice (30% of the world population's staple food) were modified to produce more food. One aspect was that the stalks were made thicker to cope with the weight of the extra surplus. The Green Revolution did boost food production and hence backed up Boserup's theory that as the population expands, new technology would be found to feed everyone. However, this technological revolution did have setbacks. HYVs were expensive to buy, meaning many small farmers couldn't compete with large TNCs. When farmers took out loans they also could not pay the money back, forcing many of them to eventually sell their land 🄱.

More recently, the Global Agriculture and Food Security Programme (GAFSP) has been set up. This works with the World Bank to finance projects that will improve food production. One example is in Rwanda, where GAFSP funding contributes to the Rwandan government's Land Husbandry, Water Harvesting and Hillside Irrigation Project (LWH) **c**. This works to increase the productivity and commercialisation of small farmers. After just 30 months the project had already reached more than 90,000 people, and yields of maize, beans and potatoes in affected areas were significantly increased. The project also looks at nutrition levels, education and gender equality by improving access to nutrition-rich vegetables such as iron-fortified beans, training communities in the construction and management of kitchen gardens and partnering with local institutions to create new financial products for smallholder farmers, particularly women **d**.

e **9/9 marks awarded**. This is an excellent answer, with two strategies being explained well — **a**, one from the relatively recent past that is well known, and **c**, another, much more recent strategy. **b** **d** In both cases there is not only a clear sense of assessment but also some evidence of linkage to other aspects of the specification, demonstrating application of knowledge and understanding. High Level 3 awarded.

Question 3

(Note how this question makes links between two separate areas of the specification, Population and the environment and Global systems.)

Evaluate the relationship between development and the incidence of non-communicable disease.
(9 marks)

e Mark scheme:

■ Level 3 (7–9 marks):

  – AO1: demonstrates detailed knowledge and understanding of concepts, processes, interactions and change. These underpin the response throughout.

  – AO2: applies knowledge and understanding appropriately and with detail. Detailed evidence of the drawing together of a range of geographical ideas, which is used constructively to support the response. Evaluation is detailed and well supported with appropriate evidence. A well-balanced and coherent argument is presented.

■ Level 2 (4–6 marks):

  – AO1: demonstrates some appropriate knowledge and understanding of concepts, processes, interactions and change. These are mostly relevant although there may be some minor inaccuracy.

  – AO2: applies some knowledge and understanding appropriately. Emerging evidence of the drawing together of a range of geographical ideas, which is used to support the response. Evaluation is clear with some support of evidence. A clear argument is presented.

- Level 1 (1–3 marks):
  - AO1: demonstrates basic/limited knowledge and understanding of concepts, processes, interactions and change. These offer limited relevance and/or there is some inaccuracy.
  - AO2: applies limited knowledge and understanding appropriately. Basic evidence of drawing together of a range of geographical ideas, which is used at a basic level to support the response. Evaluation is basic with limited support of evidence. A basic argument is presented.

Student answer

Non-communicable diseases (NCDs) are often called 'diseases of affluence' because they are associated with developed world countries. Of the 60 million global deaths each year, about 40 million, or 66%, are due to NCDs, principally cardiovascular diseases, diabetes, cancers and chronic respiratory diseases. Despite the tag of 'diseases of affluence' NCDs are the most frequent causes of death in most countries, except in Africa. Furthermore, NCD deaths are projected to continue to rise worldwide, and the greatest increase is expected to be seen in the developing world. This could of course be linked to the fact that these countries, and many people within them, are becoming more wealthy [a].

Almost 6 million people die from tobacco use each year (10% of all deaths), both from direct tobacco use and second-hand smoke. The highest incidence of smoking among men is in lower- and middle-income countries. Manufactured cigarettes represent the major form of smoked tobacco. In India alone, about 700 billion 'bidis' (a type of filter-less, hand-rolled cigarette) are consumed annually. It would appear there is no direct link to development here [b].

Insufficient physical activity is a factor more relevant to the developed world, with the Americas having the highest rates of inactivity and associated obesity, and the southeast Asia region having the lowest. At least 2.8 million people die each year as a result of being overweight or obese. The prevalence of obesity is highest in upper and middle-income countries, but it is also very high in some lower-income countries, often affecting the wealthy in those countries. India, for example, has very high levels of obesity in its rising numbers of middle classes [c].

Approximately 2.5 million people die each year from the harmful use of alcohol. While adult per capita consumption is highest in developed countries, it is nearly as high in some more populous upper-middle-income countries. It is lowest in low-income countries [d].

Two million deaths worldwide are attributable to low fruit and vegetable consumption. Most populations also consume much higher levels of salt and saturated fats than the WHO recommends. Unhealthy diet as a mortality factor is, however, rising quickly in developing nations, as their diets and attitudes to food become more Westernised (associated with rising levels of development), with fast-food outlets growing in numbers [e].

ⓔ 8/9 marks awarded. This is a very good answer, bearing in mind the requirement for linkage between two separate parts of the whole specification. The theme of relationship between development (largely economic development in this answer) and incidence of NCDs is consistently analysed by the student. ⓐ An overview is provided in the introduction, ⓑ ⓒ ⓓ ⓔ and this is followed by a step-by-step evaluation of the possible relationships for a range of NCD causes. In some cases, exemplar support is also provided — in paragraphs ⓑ and ⓒ. Furthermore, some sophistication of evaluation is provided, ⓒ pointing out variations within a population, and ⓔ recent trends. Mid-Level 3 awarded.

Question 4

With reference to a specified local area, analyse the relationships that exist between the character of a place and the health of its population. (20 marks)

ⓔ Mark scheme: see generic extended response mark scheme on pages 57–58.

> **Student answer**
>
> One case study I have studied to examine the relationship between place and health is the Isle of Man, an island located in the Irish Sea. It has a distinctive physical geography, especially in terms of its climate, and its isolation from the rest of the UK has created certain experiences for, and attitudes of, its population ⓐ.
>
> The Isle of Man's population of around 80,000 generally reflects that of the UK in terms of structure, although with a slightly higher proportion of elderly (19% over 65 as opposed to 16% in the UK). However, this percentage is expected to increase still further and healthcare provision reflects this. Cardiovascular diseases account for the largest numbers of deaths in the older age group, with the main causes of death being stroke and heart attack ⓑ.
>
> More deaths occur during the winter months as a result of the cold and damp — cold temperatures are associated with higher blood pressure, strongly associated with heart attack and stroke. The island's main average daily temperature is only 13°C ⓒ. Such problems have been tackled by reducing winter fuel poverty among older people through government subsidies and schemes such as 'Southern Befrienders'. Here, regular visits to elderly people who live alone in the south of the island, organised by local people, ensure that they are not isolated, have access to adequate nutrition and that they are keeping themselves warm.
>
> The Manx Stroke Foundation is a registered charity formed by a group of health professionals. They run a 'Stroke Club', with visiting speakers, film nights etc. to alleviate the isolation often felt by stroke sufferers and their carers. They raise funds through fairs and tombolas, and have assisted in the purchase of state-of-the-art equipment for the Stroke Wards at the island's one and only hospital: Nobles Hospital ⓓ.
>
> In addition, there are over 1,000 known cases of dementia on the island and, again, this is projected to rise, to almost double, by 2025. The island has led the UK in establishing a 'memory clinic' to aid with diagnosis, treatment and support. One of the larger residential care homes, based in Laxey, specialises in the care of Alzheimer's sufferers, although it is clear that this can only cater for a small proportion of the patients on the island ⓔ.

The island also has quite a high proportion of young people — nearly 18,000 under the age of 19, making up 24% of the population — and these are the other main users of healthcare and associated services. As with elsewhere in the UK, these young people need advice on sexually transmitted diseases and contraception. There is an additional problem that will be discussed later — alcoholism and depression, which the younger adults of the population suffer from in disproportionately high numbers. Some suggest this is due to the geographical isolation of the island, as it appears that the blame cannot be placed on unemployment. Unemployment rates on the island are very low relative to the rest of the UK. This is because of the large amount of work available in the finance industry, and the associated service industry. The rise of online betting on smartphones around the world has greatly benefited the island, as the industry exploits its low tax regimes, and there is much employment due to this activity. Money for many young adults is not in short supply here, perhaps the opposite f.

One of the biggest public health problems is obesity — a survey of IOM reception class children in 2008 suggested that 13% of girls and 17% of boys were overweight or obese. Trends show a worrying rise in obesity in this age group. Conditions such as type 2 diabetes and depression are associated with obesity, and obese children are at a higher risk of bullying. The IOM government has therefore sought to invest in preventative schemes through agencies such as the National Sports Centre (NSC) — a £20 million multi-purpose facility in Douglas. The Sports Development Unit, based at the NSC, is committed to building a strong legacy for sport on the island and has enjoyed considerable success with initiatives such as weekly 'Walk and Talk' sessions in each of the island's main towns, and the organisation of the annual Manx Youth Games, which regularly involve some 2,000 participants. In addition, the Isle of Man Children's Centre delivers a Mobile Open Access Play Scheme during the school holidays, targeting 5–11 year olds. The scheme, known as Out2Play, focuses on active play, both indoors and outdoors g.

Other problems are related to the misuse of drugs and alcohol. A Joint Drug and Alcohol Strategy has been launched, with around £200,000 per annum of government money ring-fenced for this. The suicide rate among young males in particular compares unfavourably with the UK and is thought to be tied to abuse of drugs and alcohol. There are a number of theories for the trend, including the higher levels of isolation felt by people who live on islands. In addition, island communities tend to be smaller, so people know more about each other's business and that can also be a risk factor for some people, especially when social media is at the heart of so many young people's lives today h.

Finally, in terms of wealth, the island is a relatively affluent community. Although average earnings equate roughly to those in the UK, the low tax status of the island means that many have far greater disposable incomes, and there is effectively full employment. This has led to an explosion of private health-related facilities, with roughly 20 health clubs island-wide, another 20 or so sports clubs and associations, ranging from football and rugby to yachting and kayaking, along with six riding schools. There are numerous private dental facilities, chiropodists, chiropractors along with over 30 privately run residential/retirement/nursing homes 🔲.

In conclusion, it can be seen that the physical and the socio-economic environments of the place that is the Isle of Man have greatly impacted on health and health provision. It is also possibly true that these environments have combined to generate certain attitudes of the people who live there, which also have a bearing on their health 🔲.

ⓔ 18/20 marks awarded. This is a highly detailed and focused answer. The only issue that one might have with it is that the notion of 'place' is somewhat implicitly applied, rather than being more directly stated. On the other hand, connections to health and healthcare provision are regularly stated and well analysed. 🔲 The answer begins with a clear introduction, which provides a context for the area of study. 🔲 This is followed by a discussion of one aspect of the demography of the island, and the impact it has on health. 🔲 The nature and possible impact of the climate is then examined. 🔲 🔲 The latter half of this paragraph and the subsequent two then look at strategies that are in place to deal with the health issues raised so far. It is here where perhaps there could have been more explicit statements regarding the attitudes of the people of the 'place' that is Isle of Man to the problems — their sense of community — rather than simply stating what occurs. A little manipulation of the material in the direction of the question is what is needed, but this is nitpicking. The next four paragraphs are excellent in their analysis of socio-economic aspects — 🔲 the young, 🔲 the rise of obesity, 🔲 drugs and alcohol, and 🔲 relative wealth. There is full evidence of the links and connections to geographical knowledge and understanding, and the analysis of these is coherent and relevant. 🔲 The answer ends with a neat, if brief, conclusion. Mid-Level 4 awarded.

Knowledge check answers

1 **(a) Primary effects:** these are the effects of a hazard that result directly from that event. For a volcanic eruption, these could include lava and pyroclastic flows. In an earthquake, ground shaking and rupturing are primary effects.

   (b) Secondary effects: these are the effects that result from the primary impact of the hazard event. In volcanic eruptions, these include flooding (from melting ice caps and glaciers) and lahars. In an earthquake, tsunamis and fires (from ruptured gas pipes) are secondary effects.

2 Places that were once relatively safe may have become far more at risk over time. Deforestation, for example, could result in more flooding from torrential rain associated with tropical storms and there could also be a greater risk from landslides. On the other hand, by learning from past experiences and adjusting their living conditions, people are able to reduce their levels of risk. For example, they could avoid living on sites that are at risk from storm surges, but remain within the same area.

3 Speed of onset can be crucial. For example, earthquakes come with very little warning, and the speed of onset of the ground shaking leads to maximum destruction. The 2004 Boxing Day tsunami illustrates the variation very well, with little awareness possible at Banda Aceh (Indonesia) and Thailand. However, warnings were given in many other places in the wider region, such as Sri Lanka and Kenya, and evacuation occurred.

4 Paleomagnetism refers to evidence of the Earth's magnetic field being stored within rocks as 'fossil magnetism' in that magnetic minerals align themselves with the magnetic field that was operating at the time of their formation. When magma cools as it reaches the surface, ferromagnetic minerals will behave like a compass needle and point towards the North Pole. The Earth's magnetic field has reversed many times over the last 2 billion years. The time interval for these changes has varied from 20,000 to over 10 million years. These reversals are recorded in rocks on either side of the divergent plate margin in the mid-Atlantic and the symmetry in this magnetic striping provides evidence that the plates are moving apart.

5 There is an ongoing discussion as to whether the Iceland hotspot is caused by a deep mantle plume or it originates at a much shallower depth. The plume is believed to be quite narrow, perhaps 100 km across, and extends down to at least 400–650 km beneath the Earth's surface, and possibly down to the core-mantle boundary. Studies suggest that the hotspot is only 50–100°C hotter than its surroundings, which may not be a great enough difference to drive a very buoyant plume. There is one significant difference between this hotspot and that of Hawaii: while the Hawaiian island chain shows a clear time-progressive volcanic track caused by the movement of the Pacific Plate over the Hawaiian hotspot, no such track can be seen for Iceland.

6 The frequency of a volcano's previous eruptions can be determined by its previous history if they have taken place within living memory. Alternatively, volcanologists can examine previous deposits both in the vicinity of the volcano and further afield.

7 To generate a tsunami, an earthquake has to cause a vertical displacement of the seabed. This in turn displaces water upwards, which generates a tsunami at the ocean surface. Horizontal displacements of the seabed (strike-slip faults) do not tend to generate tsunamis.

8 Tropical revolving storms have a variety of names around the world: hurricanes in the Caribbean (28% of such storms); cyclones in the Bay of Bengal (8%); typhoons in southeast Asia (43%); willy-willies in northern Australia (20%).

9 It is essential that warnings are as accurate as possible because of the high economic costs of evacuation, particularly in developed countries. Accurate predictions enable evacuation to take place smoothly and safely, and emergency services can be placed on full alert. Also, if warnings are inaccurate people may not believe the next one.

10 Managed fires are used to strip out areas of overly dense vegetation, and, as the burnt plants provide valuable minerals in the soil, they promote fresh growth. Managed fires can be used to regenerate a whole ecology or to create an ecology for a particular purpose, such as a grouse moor (for shooting birds) in northern Britain.

11 Pyrophytes are plants that have adaptations which enable them to withstand fire. This usually consists of bark that is fire-resistant. Examples of pyrophytes are the baobab tree and the acacia, both of which are typical of savanna regions. For some plants, fire is required before they can regenerate. In Australia, for example, plants such as banksia need the fire for their woody fruit to open and thus go on to regenerate.

12 Many people state that the world cannot sustain a population of 7 billion, let alone 9 billion. Others argue that it is more a case of where they are located, and how much they consume — of both food and other resources. The average person in the USA consumes almost 50 times more energy than a person in Ghana. The vast majority of greenhouse gases come from the resource-using people of the developed world. The argument is therefore whether to stop the over-consumption of resources by a minority, or reduce fertility in large parts of the developing world, especially in southern Africa, where there is under-consumption of resources. Therefore, the key factors are resource availability and resource consumption.

13 The demographic dividend is a temporary benefit. Once several decades have passed, a large number

Knowledge check answers

of older workers stop working (retire). With fewer young workers, due to a low birth rate, to fund care for the elderly, the dependency ratio begins to rise again, this time involving retirement costs rather than childcare expenses — creating a 'demographic debt'. Japan, which moved through the demographic transition ahead of other Asian nations and benefited from an economic boom in the 1960s, funds high-quality care for its current large elderly population. Some say the elderly in Japan consume more diapers (nappies) than its babies.

14 Another explanation that has been put forward for the lack of trees on the Canadian Prairie is natural fires caused by lightning, which can spread easily across the flat plains. Equally, humans could have originated some fires in prehistoric times in order to clear land for farming and improve grazing, the outcome being a generally tree-less landscape.

15 Some examples of climate-smart agriculture (CSA) are:
- superior seed varieties that can cope better with climate change
- heat-stress tolerant varieties of the main crop, such as rice and wheat
- levelling of land by lasers to improve water efficiency
- using underground pipes for irrigation, so that less water is lost through evaporation
- use of mobile telephony for accessing weather reports and advice services

16 Where irrigation water is unable to drain away due to poor drainage systems, waterlogging has taken place in the soil. The water table rises up through the soil, bringing salts with it. It is a form of human-induced salinisation.

17 (a) **Drip irrigation:** in Zimbabwe, US aid agencies have distributed drip irrigation kits to 24,000 small farmers. Designed to save labour and water, and enhance nutrition and improve food security, the average drip-irrigation kit is easy to install. It uses far less water than traditional bucket-watering.

(b) **Stone lines:** in parts of Burkina Faso, lines of stones are placed across hillsides. When the rains arrive, the water washes down the slope and is caught by the stones. Any soil carried by the water is also caught.

18 According to the WHO, there are health opportunities that depend on implementing good water practices, which include the following:
- By improving basic water supply, sanitation and hygiene systems, 4% of the global disease burden could be prevented.
- Procedures such as water safety plans (including education and the use of disinfectant) would improve and protect drinking-water quality at the community level.
- Increasing the availability of simple and inexpensive approaches to treat and safely store water at the household-level would improve water supply.

19 Médicins Sans Frontières (MSF) is a worldwide movement, with 90% of its income coming from individual donations, which the organisation says allows it to stay independent and impartial. MSF works in over 60 countries around the world, with specialist teams ready for any health emergency. MSF teams monitor epidemics on the ground continuously and are able to mount rapid emergency responses. For example, in 2014, MSF treated over 47,000 people in 16 cholera outbreaks around the world. They provided beds, plastic sheeting, oral rehydration salts and surgical equipment such as gloves and gowns. They also managed a meningitis outbreak in Niger, where as many as 350 patients were being treated on a daily basis.

20 In-migration can cause a regression within the Demographic Transition Model (DTM) such that a country that was previously in Stage 4 or Stage 5 could revert back to Stage 3. Migration tends to consist of younger adults, who have families in their 'new' country and hence the birth rate increases again. This has been shown to be the case within the UK in the last 20 years, largely due to the in-migration of young adults from eastern Europe.

21 Soaring growth rates for emerging economies, e.g. the BRIC (Brazil, Russia, India and China) and MINT (Mexico, Indonesia, Nigeria and Turkey) countries are creating hundreds of millions of new 'middle-class' consumers. In India alone, this group could grow from 160 million to 260 million by 2020. Will India be able to support the high consumption levels of this middle class? Although population change can help drive economic development, some countries could become victims of their own success if rising affluence brings challenges for energy and water consumption.

22 In 2014, four countries (Afghanistan, Iraq, Somalia and Syria) produced over 60% of the world's refugee population. Of these, Afghanistan has been the source of the most refugees in recent years, though Syria has emerged as a significant source of refugees since the outbreak of internal conflict in 2011.

23 Positive feedback loops may also cause serious environmental problems, as they can cause resource depletion. For example, although the use of fossil fuel energy has increased our capacity to produce food, climate scientists say that it is creating a rise in global temperatures and a shift in rainfall patterns (due to the emission of greenhouse gases), which might negatively impact on the food production of much of the world's existing farmland.

24 By 2025 the population of India is expected to surpass that of China. Thereafter, India's population is projected to continue growing for several decades, to 1.5 billion in 2030 and 1.7 billion in 2050, while the population of China is expected to remain fairly constant at 1.4 billion until the 2030s, after which it is expected to slightly decrease. Nigeria's population is growing the most rapidly. Consequently, Nigeria is projected to have the third-largest population in the world by 2050.

Note: Page numbers in **bold** indicate key term definitions.